W9-DEF-704

Picture Perfect Dictionary 1

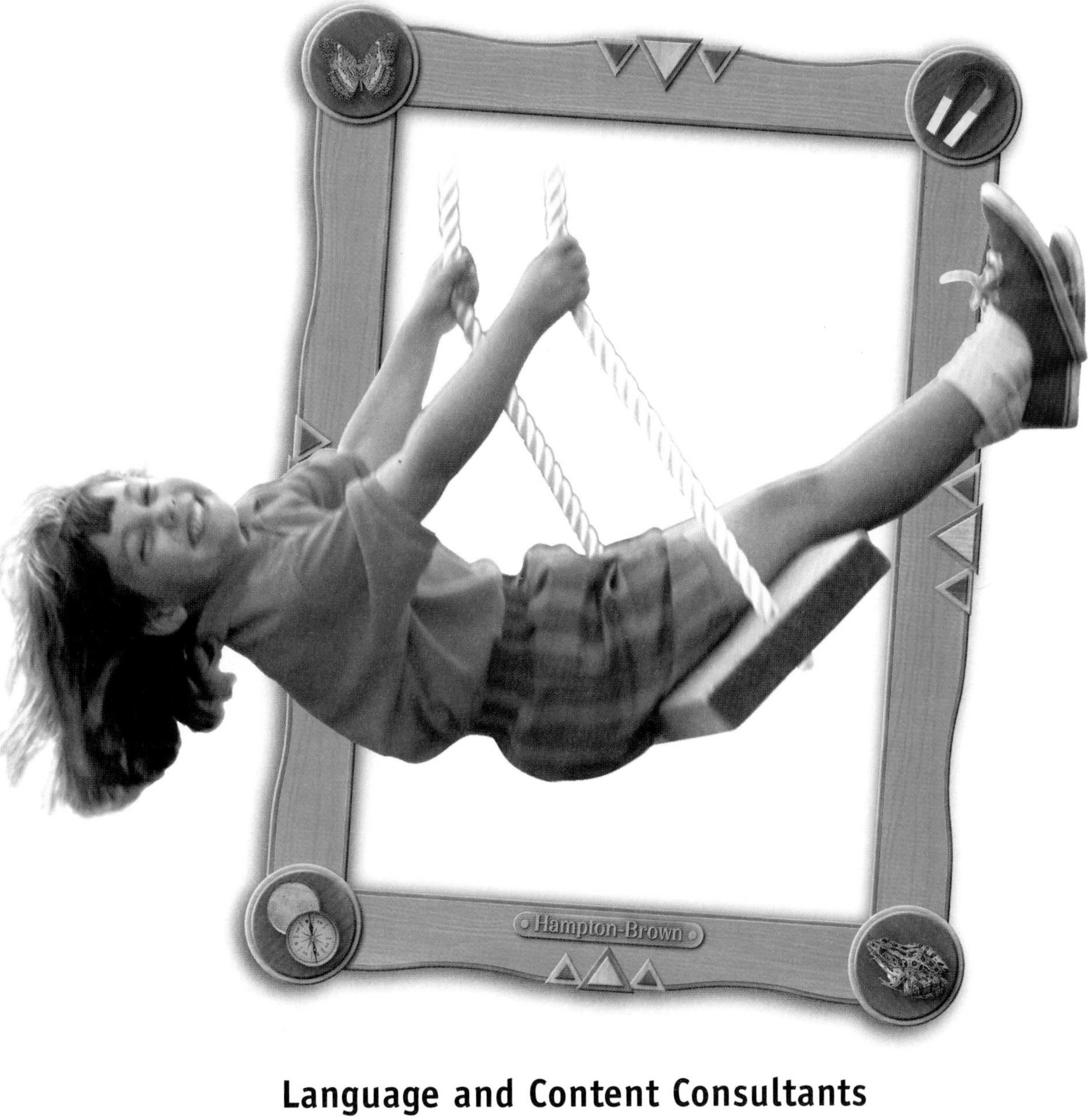

Language and Content Consultants
JoAnne Johnson • Madeleine Joe Lee • J. Blanca O. López

About the Consultants

JoAnne Johnson
Primary Classroom Teacher
Woodbine Elementary School
Cicero School District
Cicero, Illinois

Madeleine Joe Lee
Literacy Coach
Hawthorne Year Round School
Oakland Unified School District
Oakland, California

J. Blanca O. López
Bilingual Urban Systemic Initiative Mentor
Kindergarten–Grade 6
Ysleta Independent School District
El Paso, Texas

Credits

Hampton-Brown
Editorial: Lisa Baehr, Mary Borgia, Fredrick Ignacio, Sheron Long, Sarita Chávez Silverman
Art/Design: Jeri Gibson, Ray Godfrey
Production: Cathy Blake, Andrea Carter, Curtis Spitler

Brown Publishing Network, Inc.
Editorial: Elinor Chamas, Jean MacFarland
Art/Design: Jennifer Angell, Trelawney Goodell, Nicole Schildcrout, Camille Venti
Photo Research: Libby Taft, Nina Whitney
Production: Diane Carnevale, Cheryle D'Amelio, Anthony Fisher, Kathleen Spahn

Hampton-Brown
P.O. Box 223220
Carmel, California 93922
(800) 333–3510

Printed in the United States of America.

0-7362-0181-5
02 03 04 05 06 07 10 9 8 7 6 5

Contents

Aa add *to* awake 5
Bb baby *to* buy 9
Cc cab *to* cylinder 16
Dd dance *to* dusty 25
Ee each *to* experiment 30
Ff face *to* funny 33
Gg garbage *to* guide 39
Hh half *to* husband 43
Ii ice *to* island 47
Jj jar *to* jungle 49
Kk keep *to* know 51
Ll lake *to* lunch 53
Mm machine *to* music 56
Nn name *to* number 61
Oo observe *to* order 65
Pp pack *to* puzzle 69
Qq question *to* quite 77
Rr race *to* rush 78
Ss sack *to* syllable 84
Tt take *to* type 95
Uu umbrella *to* United States 99
Vv valentine *to* vehicle 101
Ww walk *to* write 103
Xx X-ray *to* xylophone 107
Yy yard *to* yesterday 108
Zz zero *to* zoo 109

Word-Finder Index 112

Special Expanded Entries

• More to See! • More to Learn!

animal 6
ant 8
bird 12
body 13
build 15
calendar 16
career 18
clothing 22
desert 26
family 33
farm 34
feelings 36
forest 37
grocery 40
grow 42
home 44
house 45
insect 48
jungle 50
make-believe 57
mammal 57
measure 59
money 60
neighborhood 62
number 64
opposite 66
orchestra 68
park 71
pet 73
plant 75
rain forest 78
reptile 79
restaurant 80
school 85
sea 86
seashore 88
senses 89
tool 97
United States 100
vehicle 102
weather 104
zoo 110

add

He can **add** these numbers.

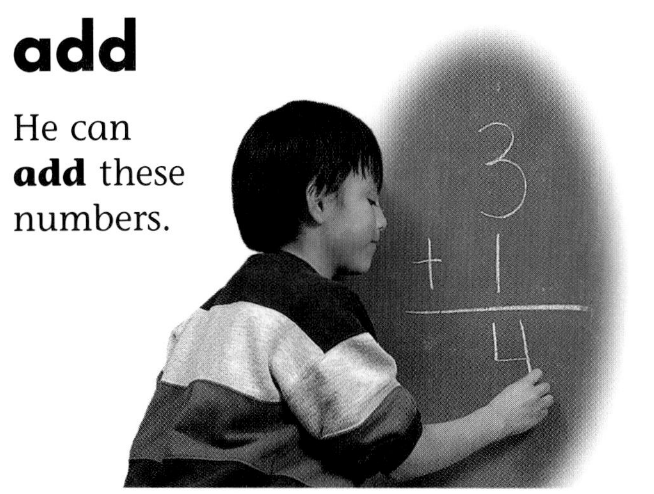

address

An **address** tells where you live.

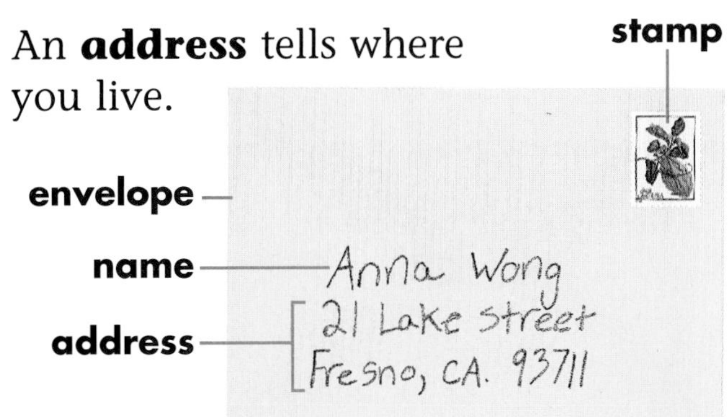

adult

There is one **adult** in this picture.

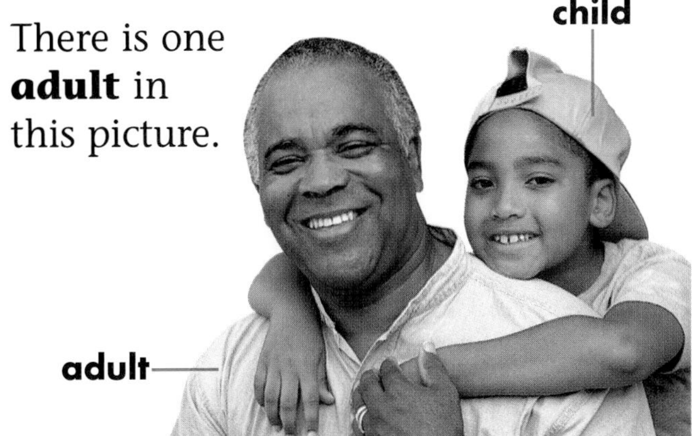

afternoon

Music time is after lunch. We sing every **afternoon**.

age

Your **age** changes every year.

age 5 age 9 age 14

alike

The children are dressed **alike**.

alphabet

This **alphabet** has 26 letters.

Aa Bb Cc Dd Ee Ff Gg
Hh Ii Jj Kk Ll Mm Nn
Oo Pp Qq Rr Ss Tt Uu
Vv Ww Xx Yy Zz

capital letter lowercase letter

A B C D E F G H I J K L M N O P Q R S T U V W X Y Z

animal

There are many different kinds of **animals**. Some live with people. Others do not.

Animal Families

pup fox

kangaroo

joey

turtle baby turtle

bear

cubs

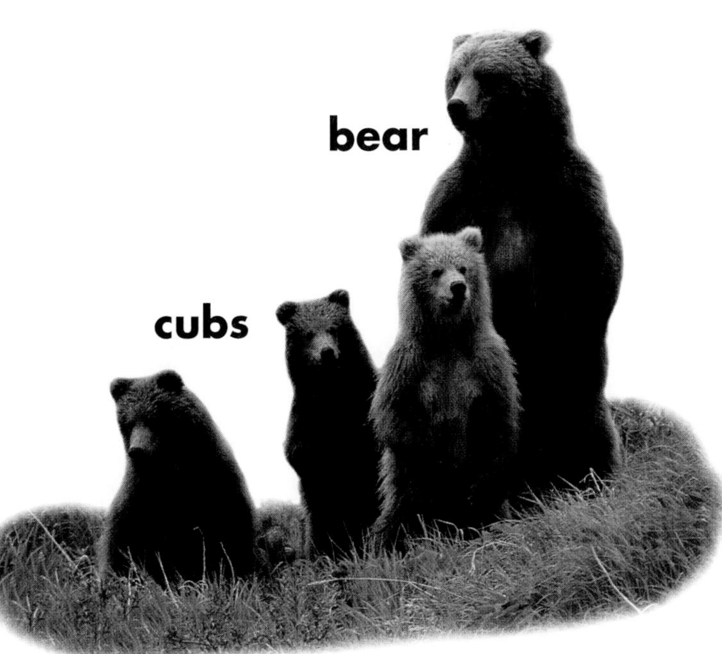

Birds live in a nest.

Snakes live in a hole.

Frogs live in a pond.

Foxes live in a den.

Deer live in the woods.

A B C D E F G H I J K L M N O P Q R S T U V W X Y Z

ant

An **ant** is a tiny insect.

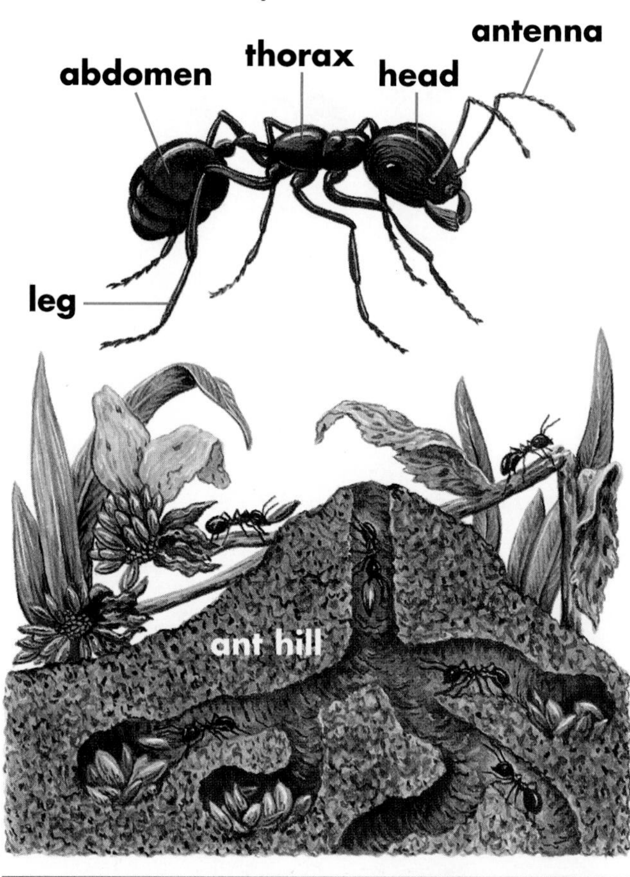

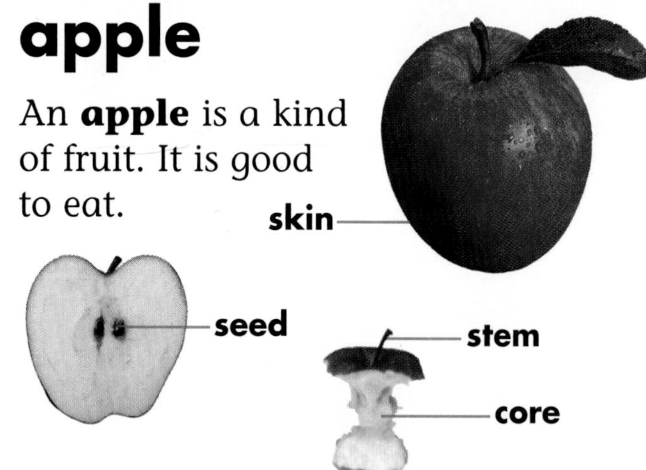

apple

An **apple** is a kind of fruit. It is good to eat.

around

My mom puts her arms **around** me.

asleep

The girl is **asleep**.

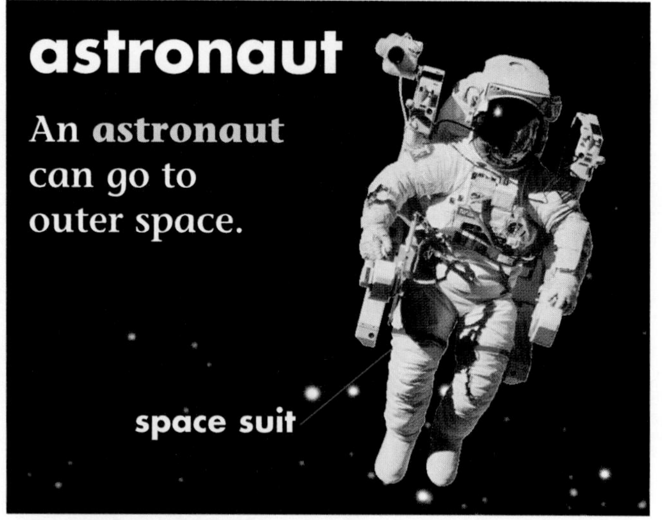

astronaut
An astronaut can go to outer space.
space suit

author

Dr. Seuss wrote this story. He is an **author**.

title
Green Eggs and Ham
By Dr. Seuss
author

awake

Kendra had a nap. Now she is **awake**.

Bb

baby

This **baby** is happy.

ball

You can throw or kick a **ball**. It's fun to play with a ball.

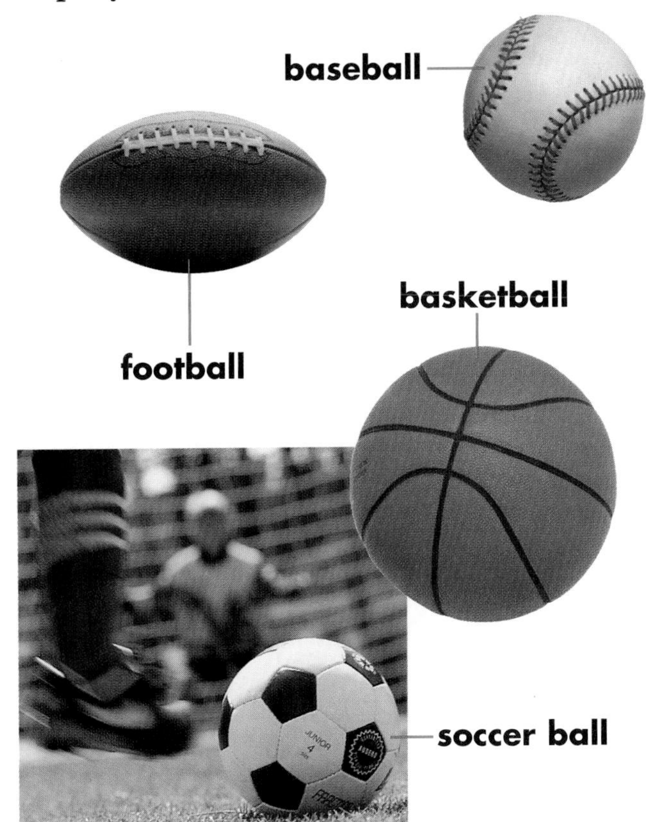

band

A **band** plays music. You can listen and dance to a band.

bank

1. You can save money in a piggy **bank**.

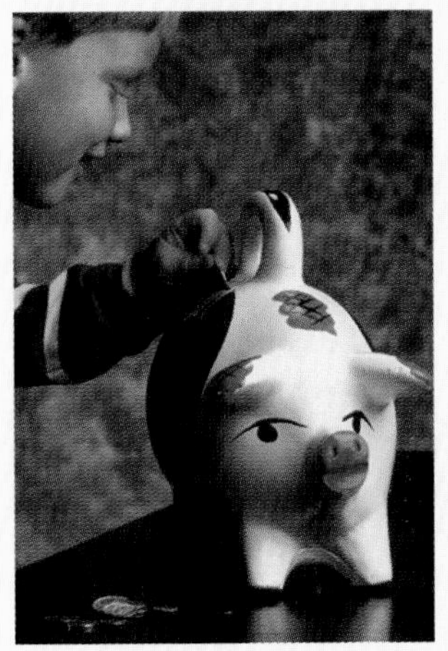

2. The boys walk along the **bank** of the river.

basket

A **basket** is a good place to keep things.

A B C D E F G H I J K L M N O P Q R S T U V W X Y Z

bathroom

This is a **bathroom**. It has a sink, a toilet, and a bathtub.

beat

You **beat** a drum with a stick.

beautiful

The rainbow is **beautiful**. We love to see it in the sky.

rainbow

bedroom

This is a **bedroom**. It has a bed for sleeping.

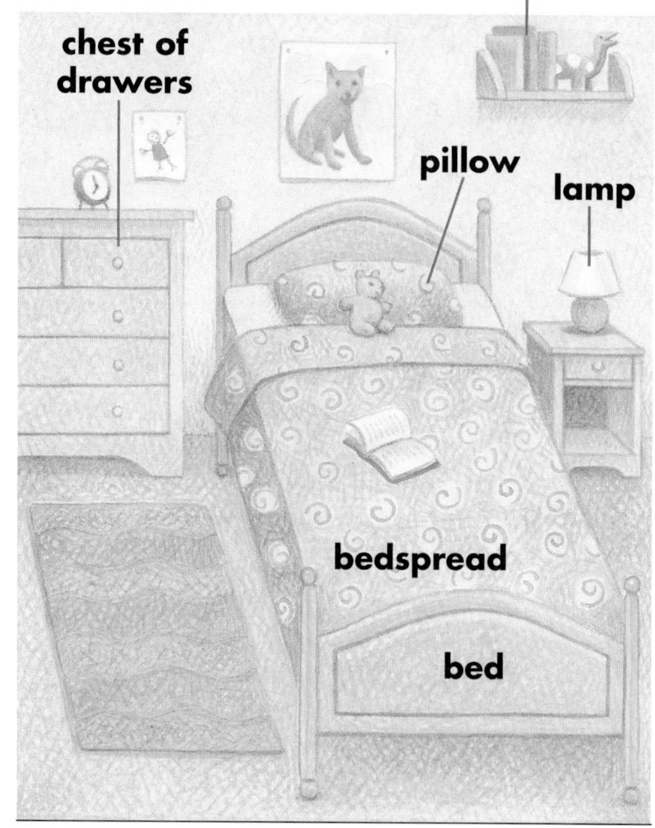

begin

Pam will **begin** by drawing a circle.

beginning

This is the **beginning** of the story. I'll start to read here.

behind

Jack is **behind** the snowman.

beside

Noor is **beside** the snowman.

between

The snowman is **between** Jack and Noor.

bicycle

A **bicycle** is sometimes called a bike.

big

The water buffalo is **big**.
The bird is little.

bill

❶ The dollar **bill** is paper money.

❷ The **bill** on a cap keeps the sun off your face.

bird

A **bird** is an animal with feathers. There are many different kinds of birds.

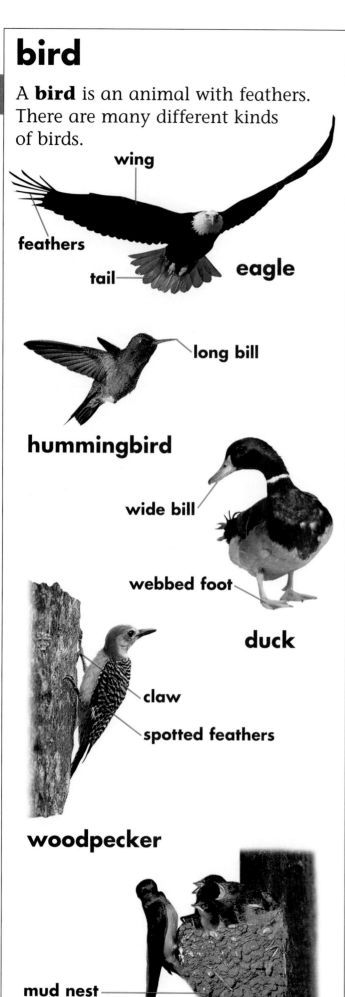

wing

feathers

tail

eagle

long bill

hummingbird

wide bill

webbed foot

duck

claw

spotted feathers

woodpecker

mud nest

barn swallow

birthday

Reza has a **birthday** today. He is 8 years old.

bite

You can **bite** a juicy apple.

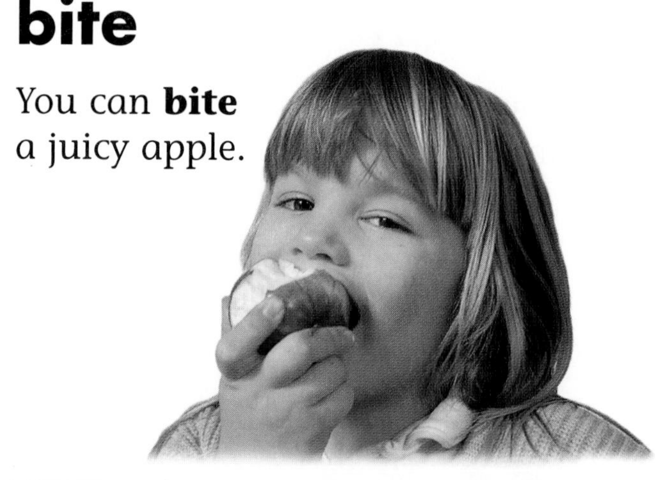

blow

It's fun to **blow** bubbles.

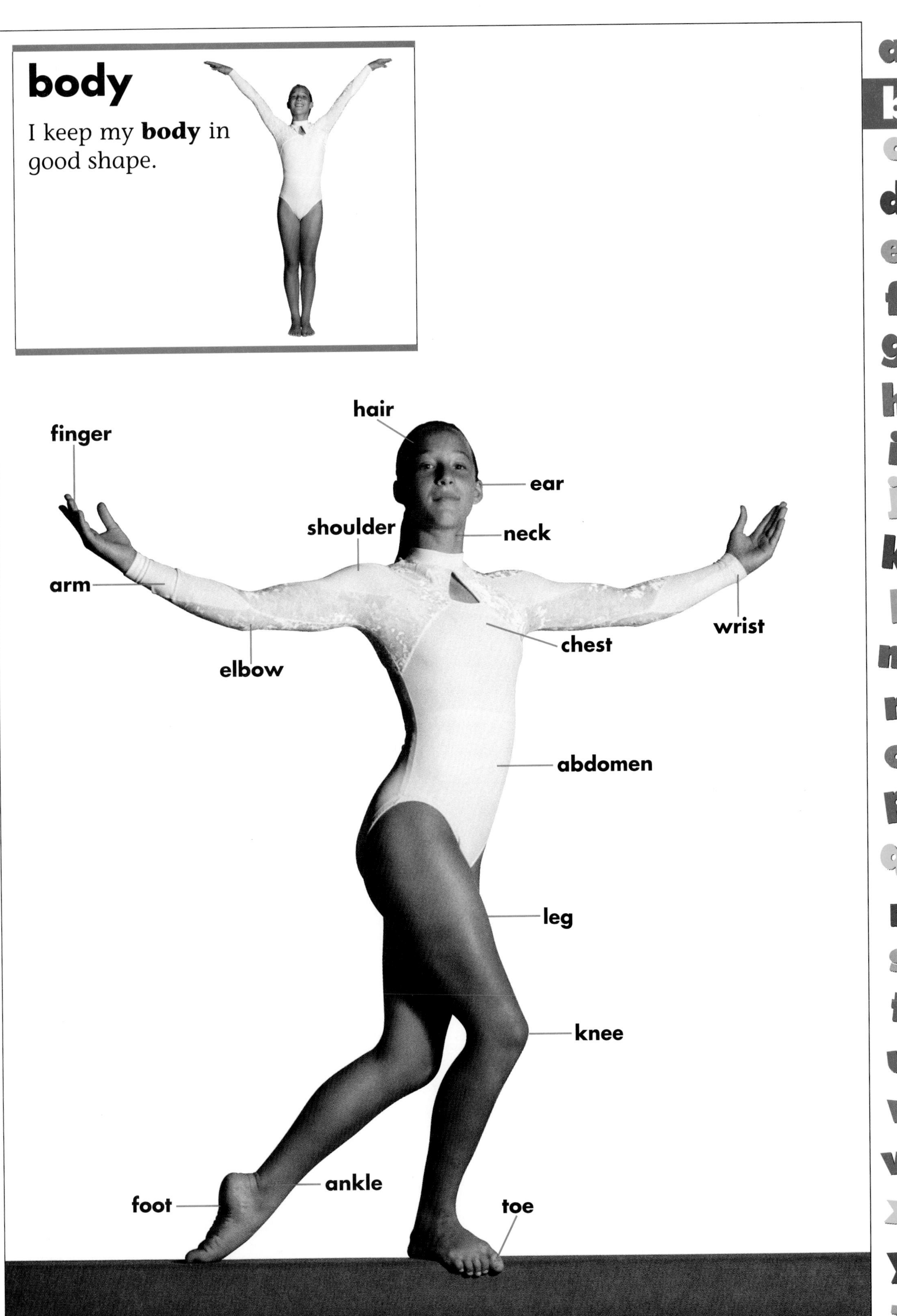

body

I keep my **body** in good shape.

hair
finger
ear
shoulder
neck
arm
wrist
chest
elbow
abdomen
leg
knee
ankle
foot
toe

A B C D E F G H I J K L M N O P Q R S T U V W X Y Z

book

Children like to read this **book**.

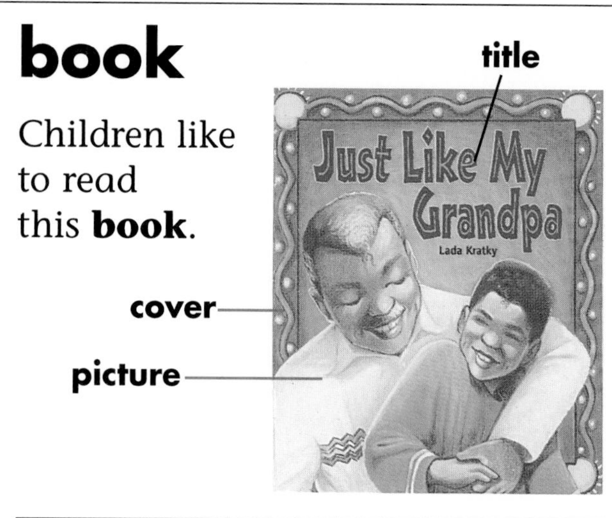

bottom

The red block is at the **bottom** of the tower.

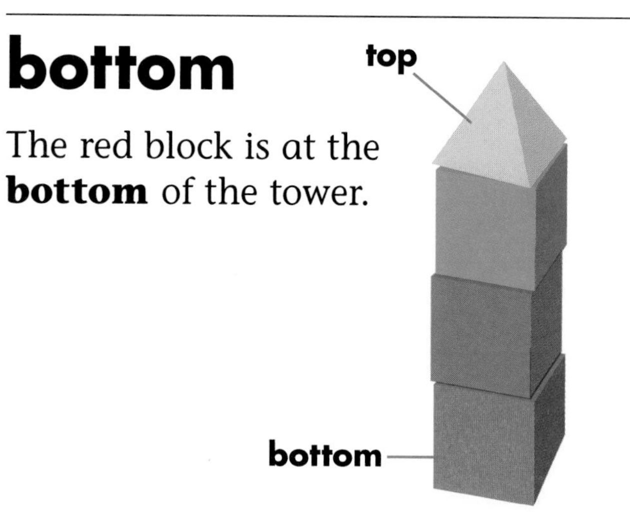

bowl

Lili eats soup from a **bowl**.

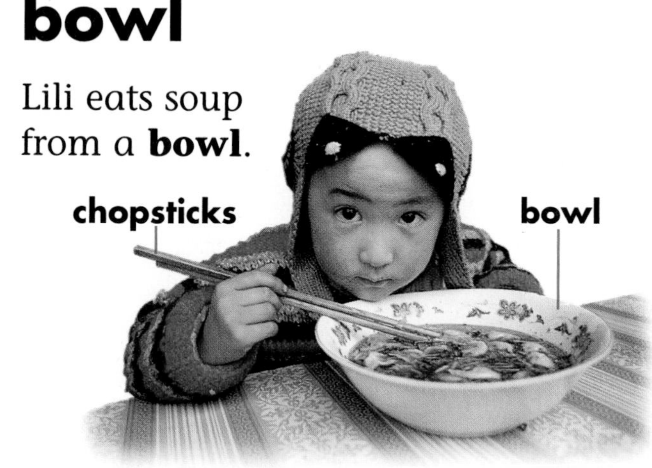

box

Mai keeps things in a **box**.

boy

Sam is a **boy**. Juan is a man.

break

The children **break** the piñata.

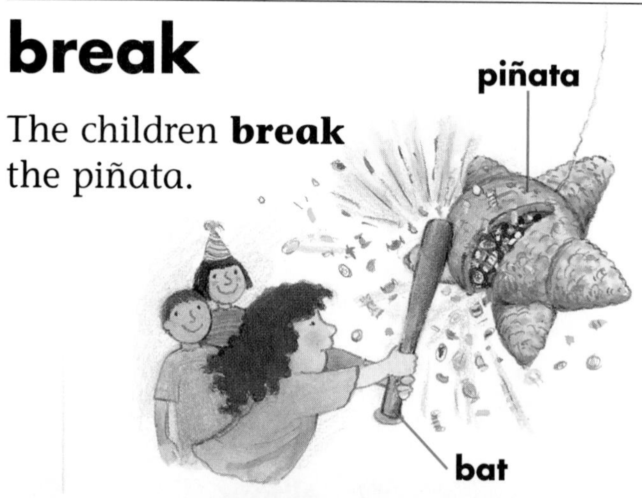

bright

The moon looks **bright** tonight. The sky is dark.

bring

Dad will **bring** the cookies.

build

People **build** many things.
They use tools.

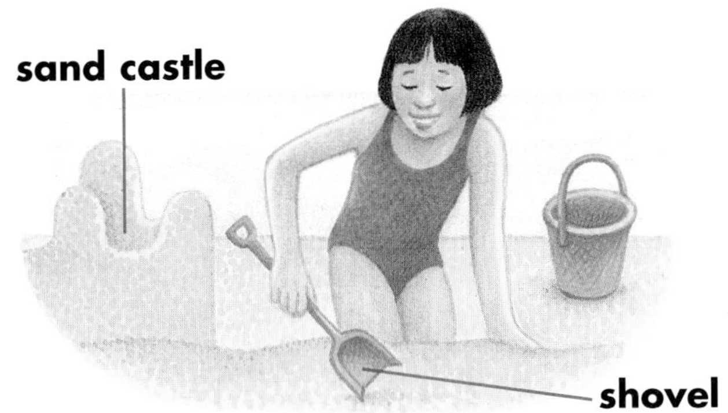

building

This is an
office **building**.

burn

The candle can
burn. The flame
is hot.

flame

wick

candle

bus

The children ride the **bus** to school.

button

This coat has
lots of **buttons**.

buy

Lien will **buy** a balloon.

cab

You pay money to ride in a **cab**, or taxi.

cafeteria

We eat lunch in the school **cafeteria**.

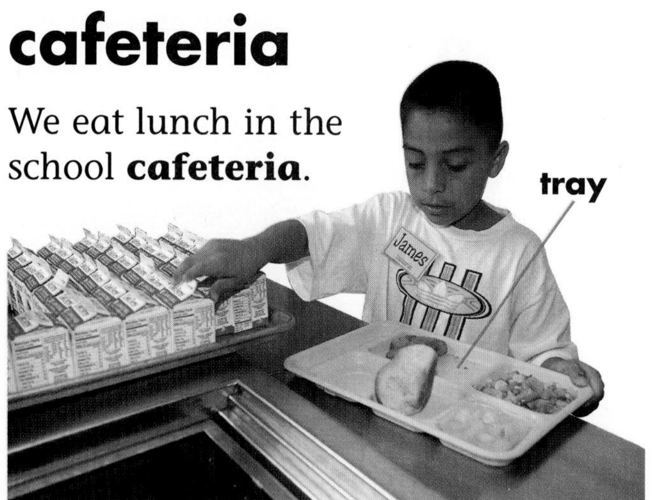

calculator

You can use a **calculator** to add numbers.

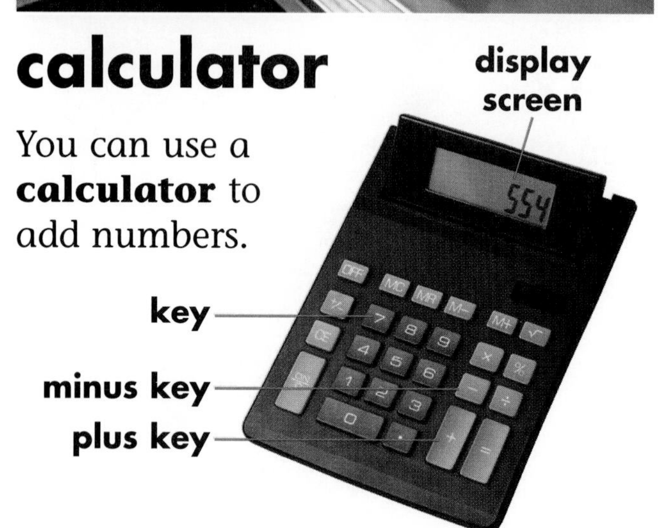

calendar

A **calendar** shows the months of the year:

January	**July**
February	**August**
March	**September**
April	**October**
May	**November**
June	**December**

January

Sunday	Monday	Tuesday	Wednesday	Thursday	Friday	Saturday
				1	2	3
4	5	6	7	8	9	10
11	12	13	14	15	16	17
18	19	20	21	22	23	24
25	26	27	28	29	30	31

days of the week

one month

one week

call

Call 911 if you need help!

camp

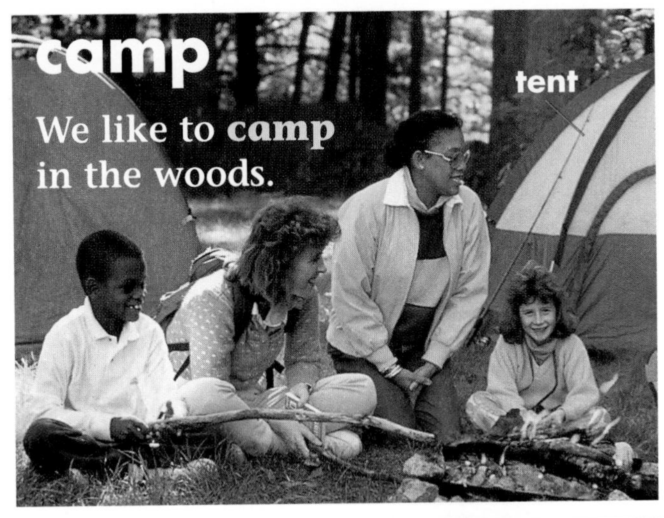

We like to **camp** in the woods.

can

1. Let's put the **can** in this bin.
2. We **can** recycle newspapers, too.

capital

The **capital** of Florida is Tallahassee.

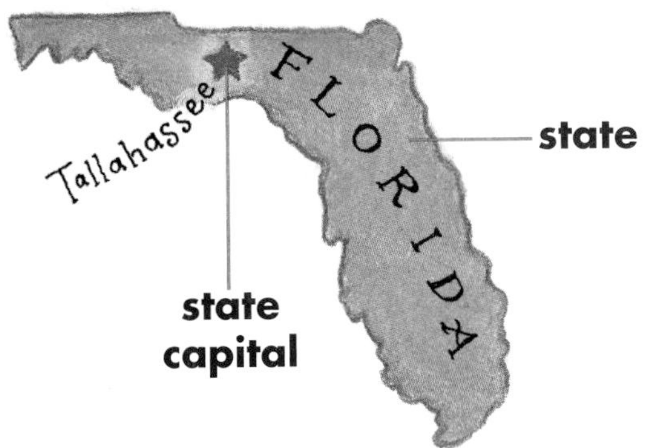

car

Would you like to ride in this **car**?

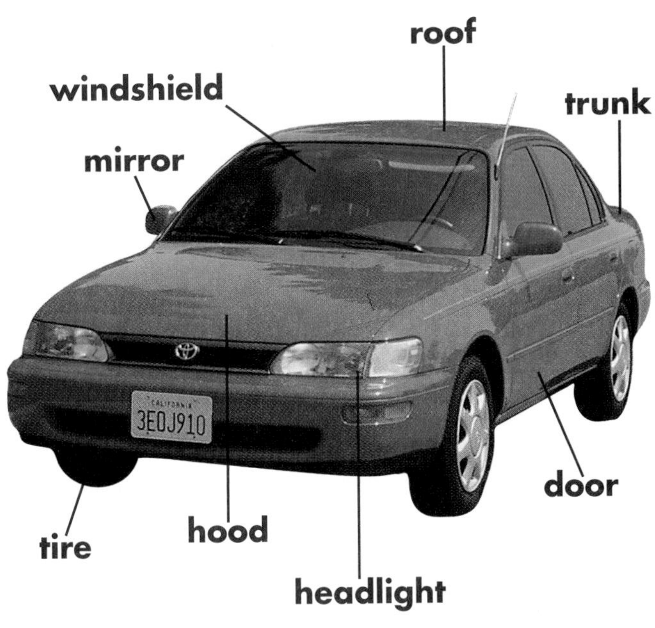

card

I made a birthday **card** for my grandmother.

care

A pet needs special **care** every day.

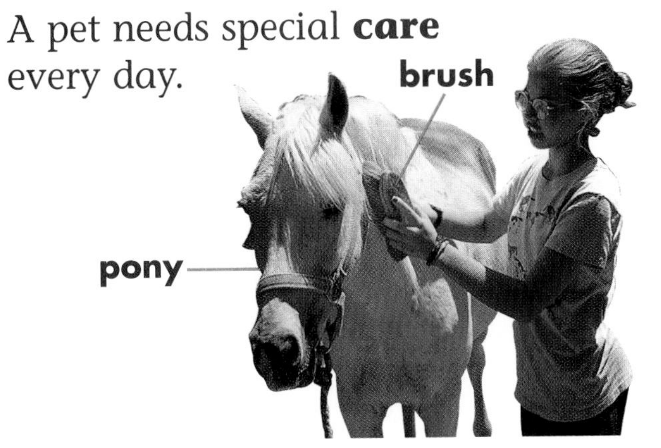

career

This man chose a fine **career**. He is a teacher.

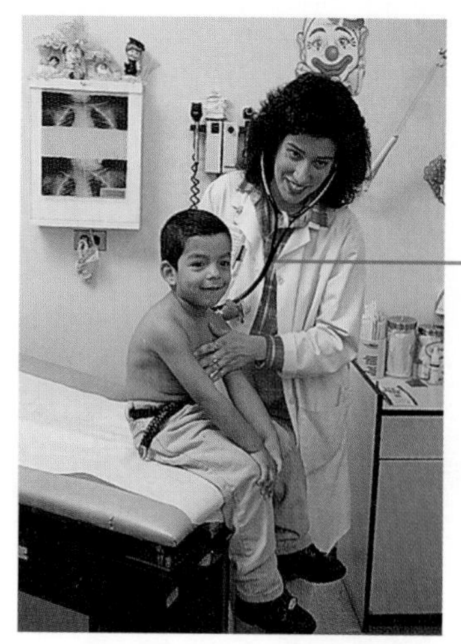

doctor

bus driver

pilot

carpenter

barber

TV reporter

architect

firefighter

letter carrier

cook

What are these workers doing?

The construction worker is driving a dump truck.

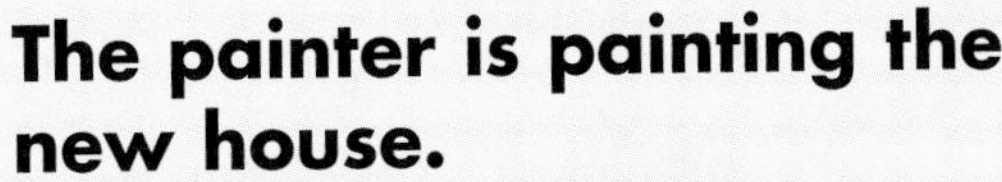

The painter is painting the new house.

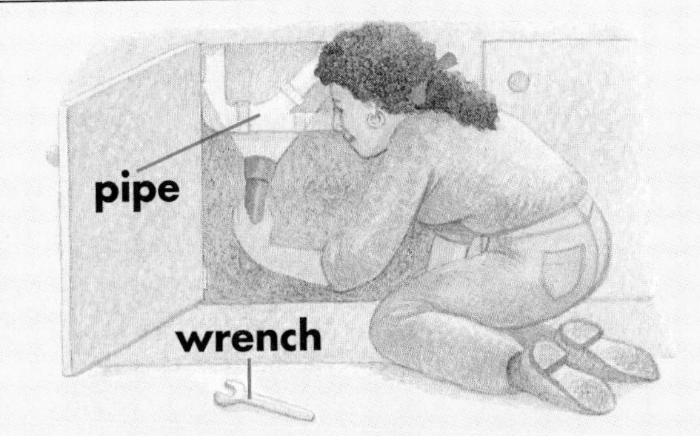

The plumber is fixing the broken pipe.

The librarian is checking out a book.

cargo

Ships carry **cargo** from one place to another.

catch

Jessie can **catch** the ball.

cause

Why is it so wet? The rain is the **cause**.

celebration

Everyone has fun at the birthday **celebration**.

change

1. Anna paid one dollar. She got 25 cents in **change**.
2. Tadpoles **change** into frogs.

character

Sam will act in a play. His **character** is the dragon.

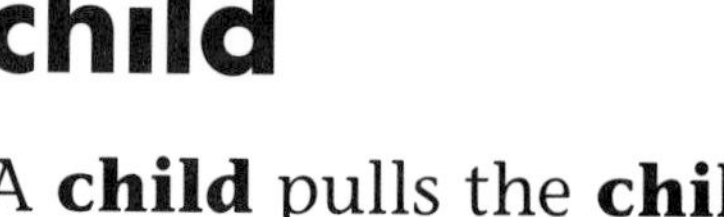

child

A **child** pulls the **children**.

circle

You can trace the round shape of a **circle**.

circus

It's fun to go to the **circus**.

city

A **city** is full of people and buildings.

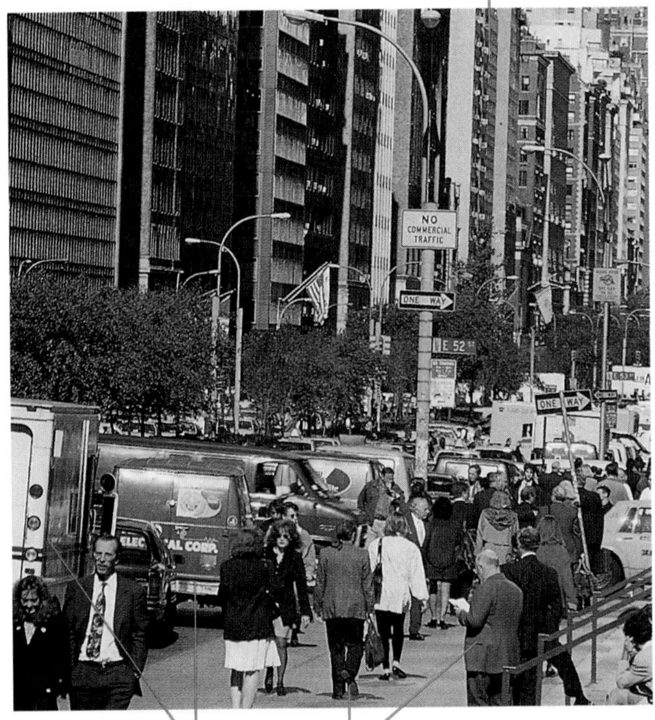

classify

You can **classify** these blocks. You can put them into groups.

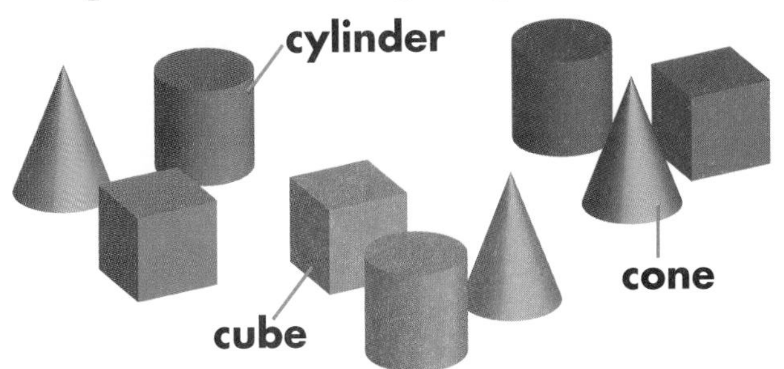

clay

People use **clay** to make pots.

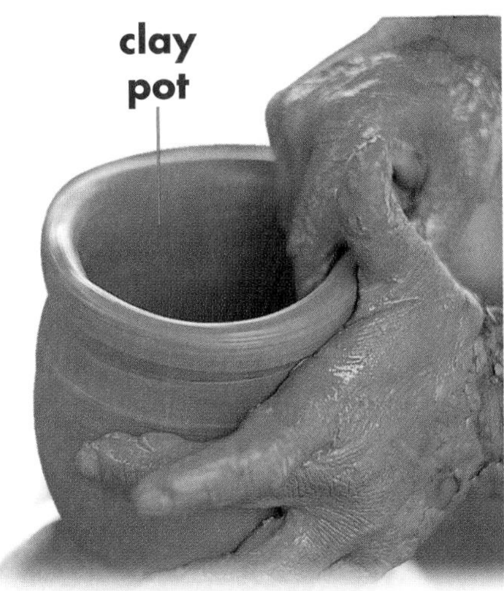

clean

Dawn likes to **clean** the van with soap and water.

climb

They can **climb** a ladder in the gym.

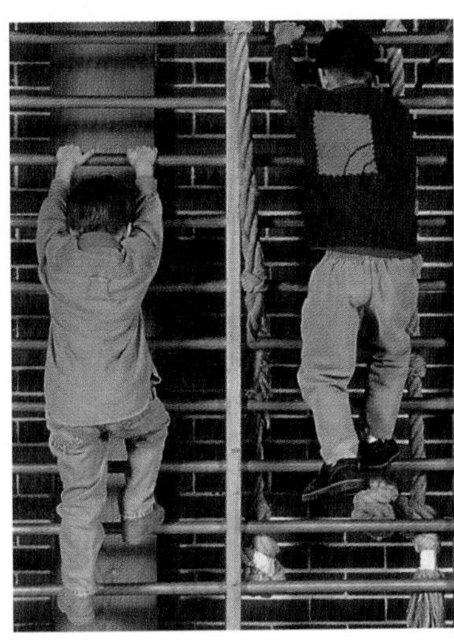

a b c d e f g h i j k l m n o p q r s t u v w x y z

clothing

Every day you choose **clothing** to wear to school.

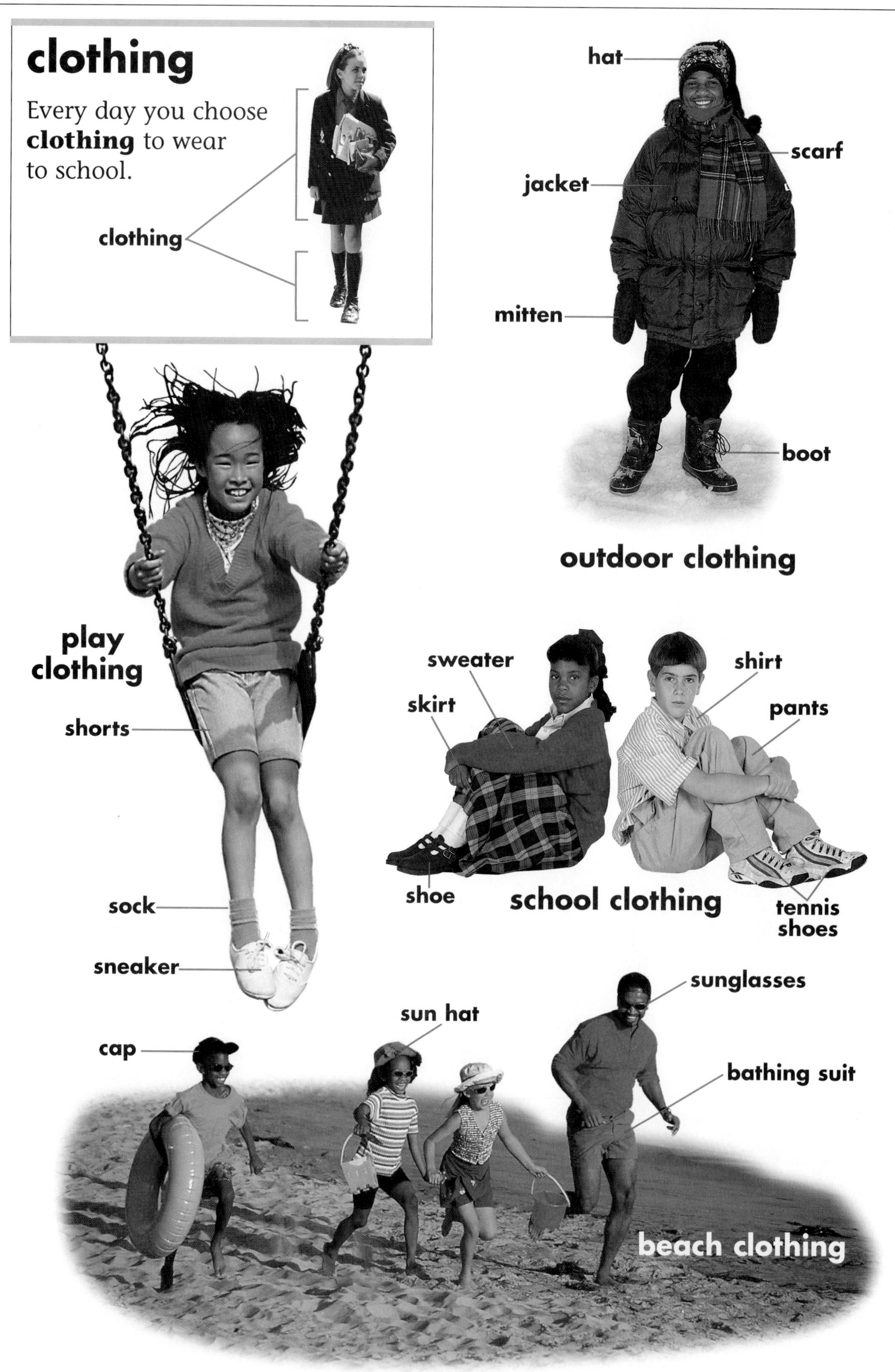

color

You can make the **color** green. Just mix blue with yellow.

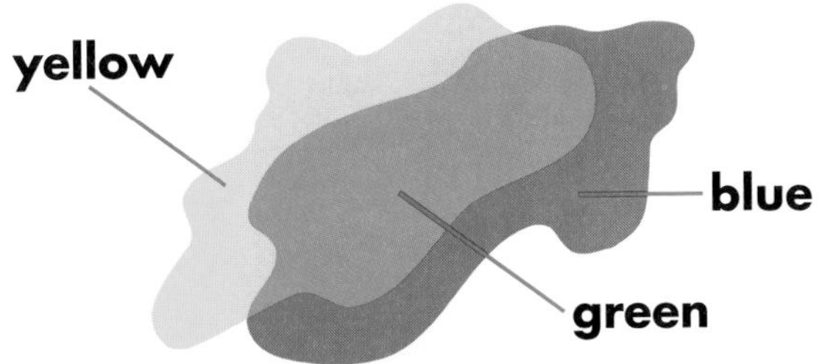

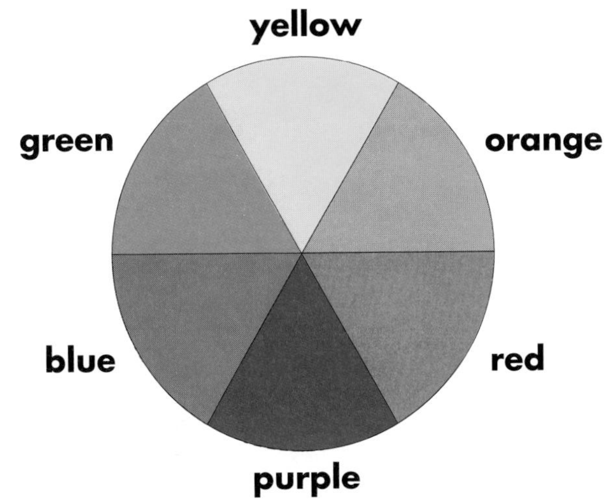

come

Please **come** to my birthday party.

compare

Let's **compare** these fruits. One is yellow. One is green. Both are sour.

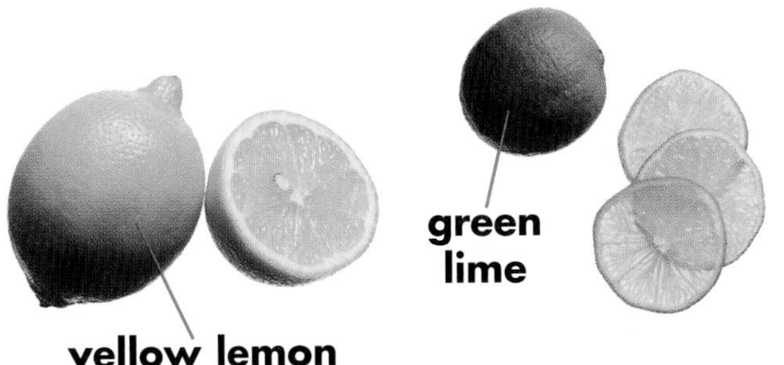

computer

You can use a **computer** to do homework.

continent

South America is a **continent**. You can see it on a map.

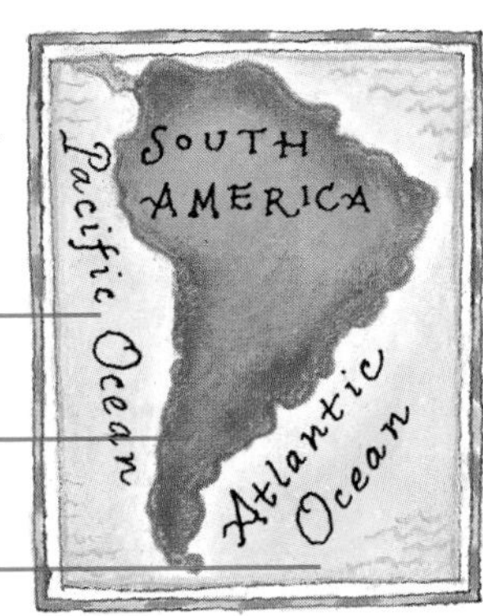

cook

My dad loves to **cook**.

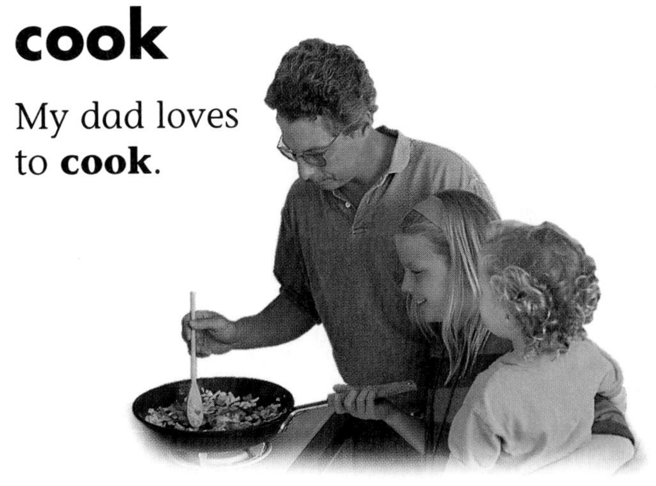

count

Bev likes to **count** her pennies.

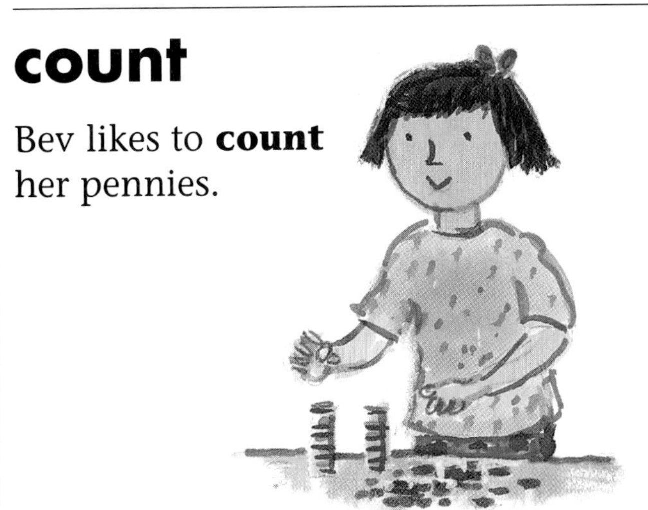

a b c d e f g h i j k l m n o p q r s t u v w x y z

A B C D E F G H I J K L M N O P Q R S T U V W X Y Z

country

1. Brazil is a **country** in the continent of South America.

2. Our home in the **country** is far away from the city.

cousin

Rosa is my **cousin**.

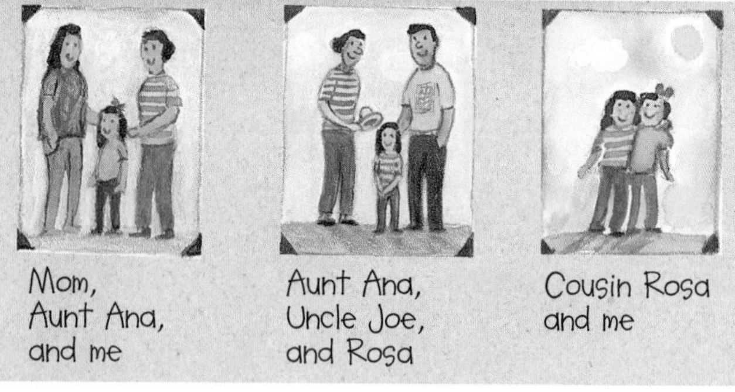

Mom, Aunt Ana, and me
Aunt Ana, Uncle Joe, and Rosa
Cousin Rosa and me

cube

A number **cube** has six sides.

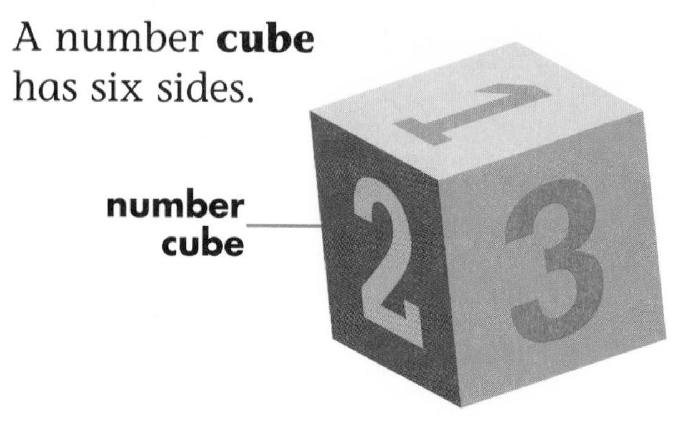

curly

My friend has **curly** hair.

customer

Ray is a **customer** at the toy store. He is buying a toy car.

cut

You can use scissors to **cut** things.

cylinder

This can is in the shape of a **cylinder**.

dance

This is a special **dance**.

dangerous

It is **dangerous** to cross the street when the light is red.

dark

When it gets **dark**, the lights on the bridge go on.

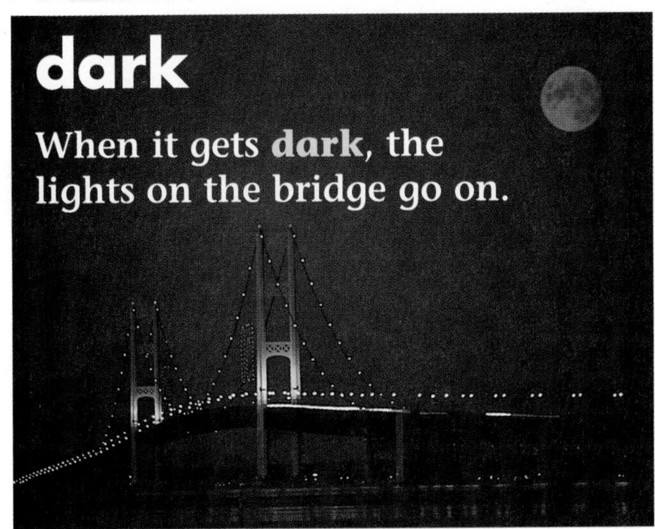

daughter

These parents have one **daughter**.

day

The sun is up during the **day**. It goes down at night.

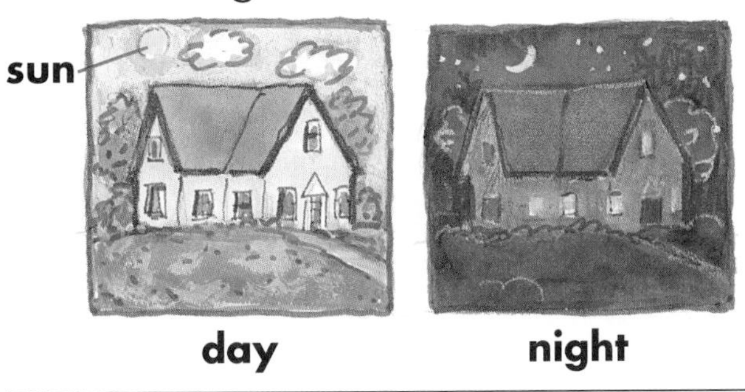

decorate

It is fun to **decorate** a piñata.

deep

The dog dug a **deep** hole in the dirt.

desert

The **desert** is a dry place.
It can be very hot in the day.
It can be very cold at night.

Animals and Plants of the Desert

mule deer

beaver-tail cactus

desert marigold

antelope squirrel

yucca

antelope jack rabbit

tarantula

desert king snake

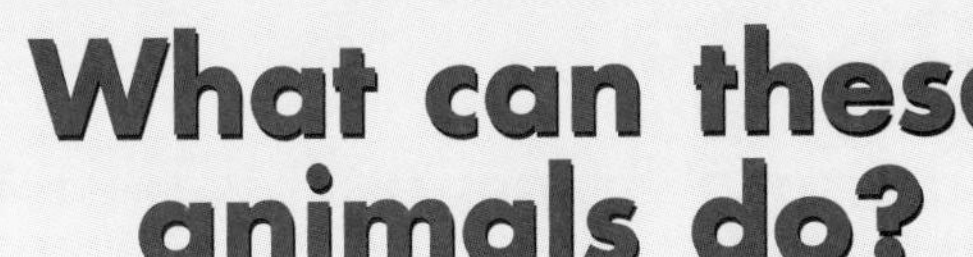

What can these animals do?

A sidewinder can slide along the sand.

This tortoise can burrow in the ground.

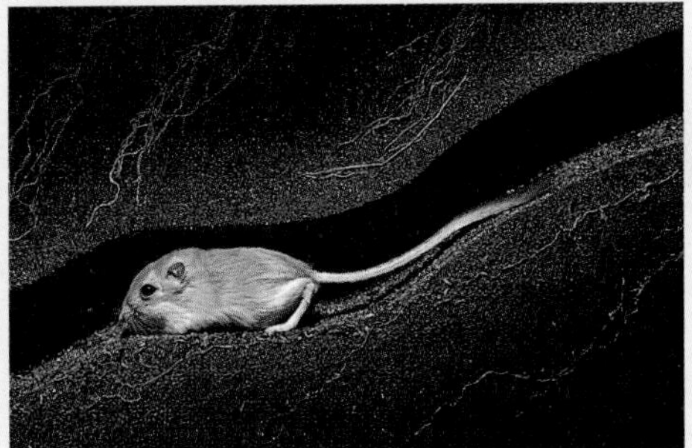

A kangaroo rat can crawl in a tunnel under the ground.

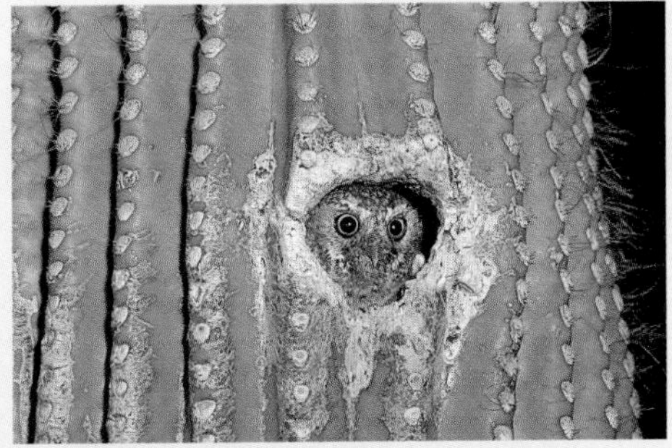

An elf owl can live inside a cactus.

A B C D E F G H I J K L M N O P Q R S T U V W X Y Z

diamond

The **diamond** shapes in this pattern are blue and red.

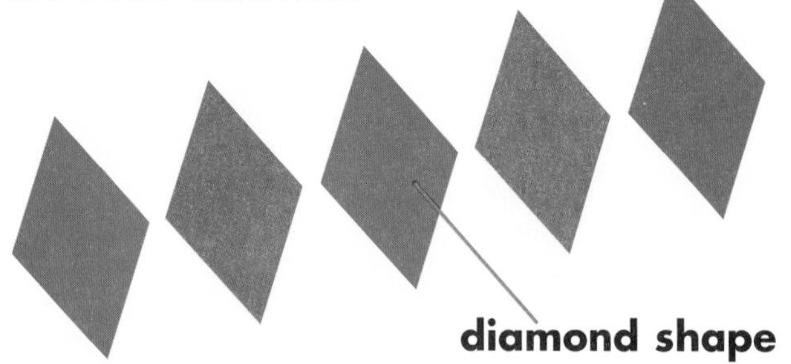

difference

Take 2 away from 6. What is the **difference**?

different

The shoelaces are **different** colors.

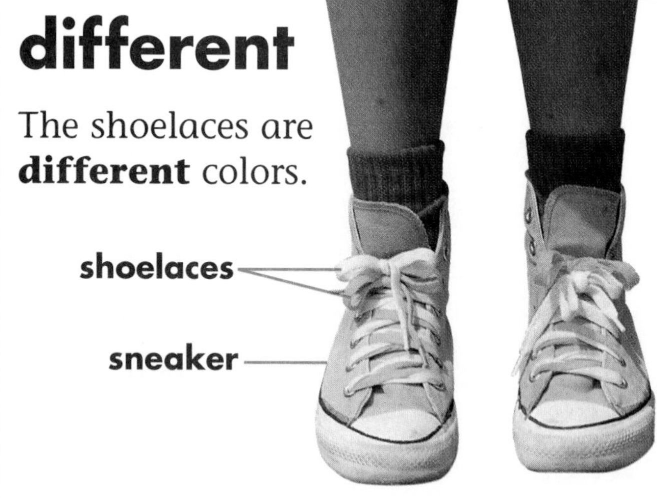

dig

You need to **dig** a hole to plant a flower.

dinner

Tenkai eats **dinner** with his family.

directions

1. You need to read the **directions** for the game.

2. North, south, east, and west are **directions**.

divide

You can **divide** the pizza into pieces.

do

We **do** many art projects in school.

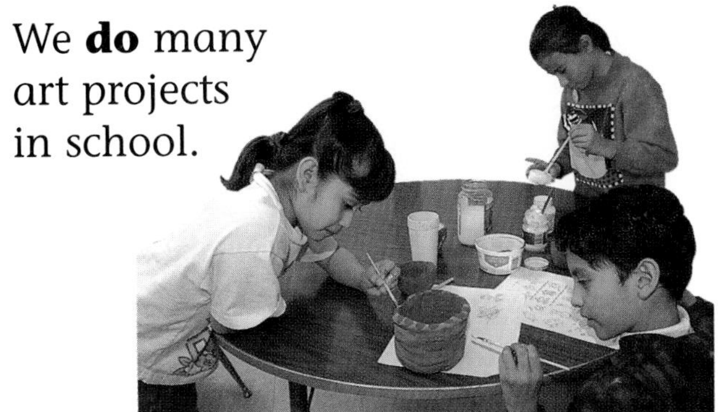

dock

The boat is near the **dock**.

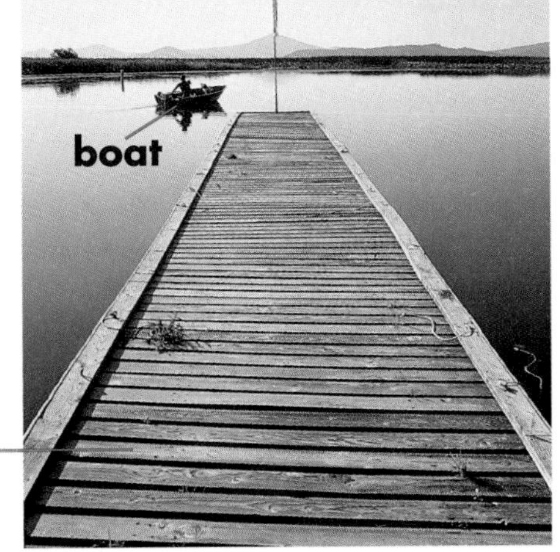

double

The number of apples is **double** the number of bananas.

draw

Len can **draw** a picture of a face.

drink

I **drink** milk every day.

drop

Be careful! You might **drop** your books!

dry

The garden needs water. It is very **dry**.

dusty

These books are **dusty**. We need to clean them.

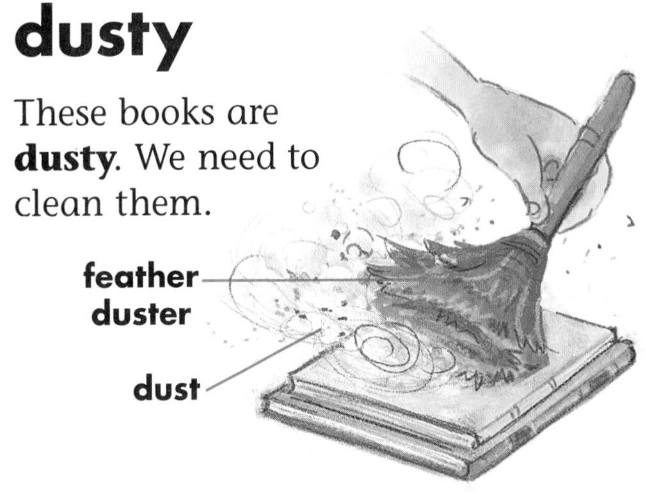

Ee

each

The teacher gives **each** student a book.

early

We arrived at the play one hour **early**.

earn

You can do a job to **earn** money.

easy

This math problem is **easy** for me.

eat

Ice cream cones are fun to **eat**.

edge

Please don't put your glass near the **edge** of the table.

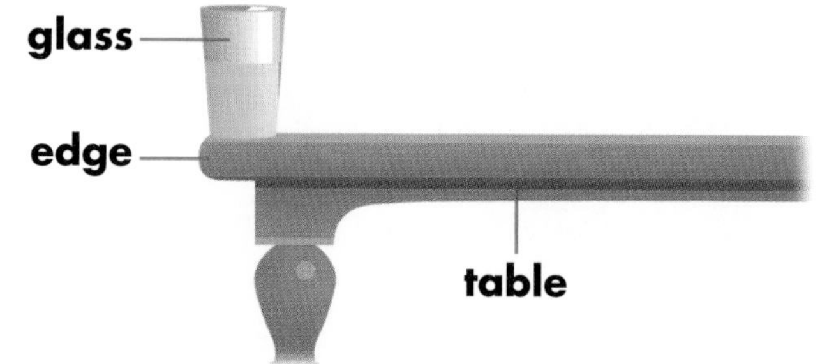

effect

The bike runs over a nail. The **effect** is a flat tire.

cause

effect

egg

You can eat a fried **egg** for breakfast.

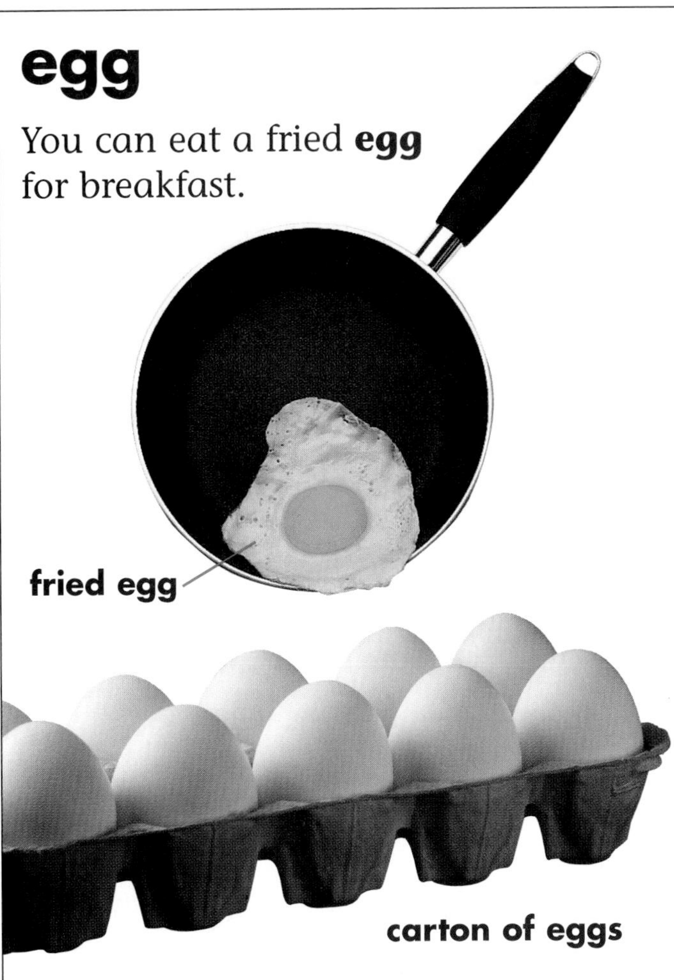

end

❶ The **end** of the book is on page 75.

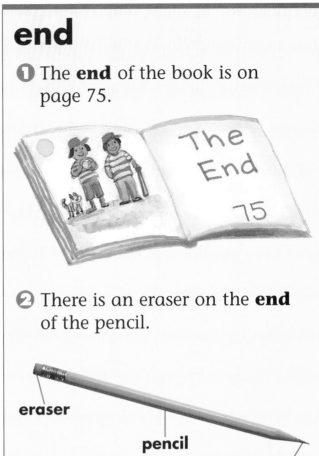

❷ There is an eraser on the **end** of the pencil.

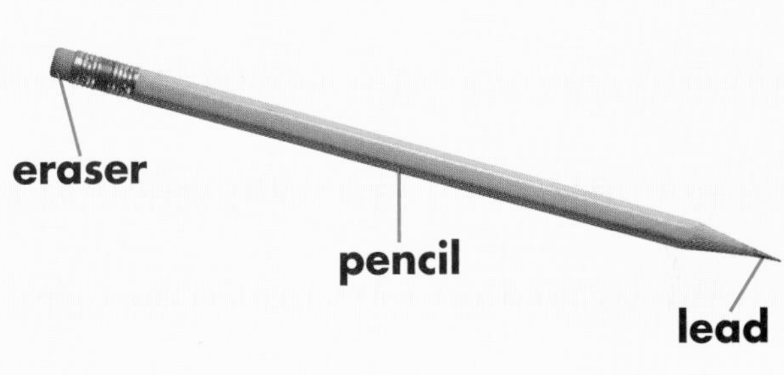

electricity

You need **electricity** to make the lights go on.

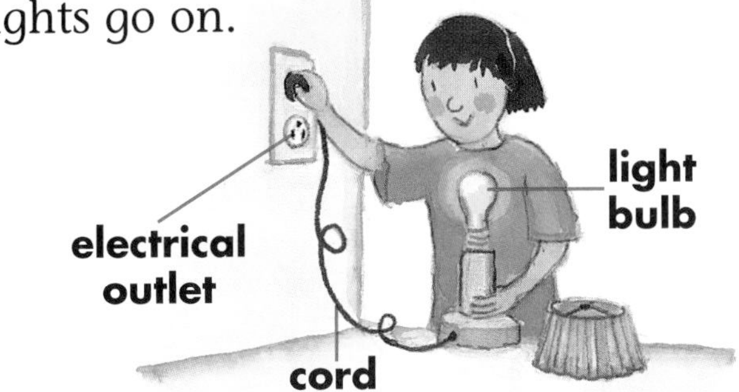

energy

Energy from the wind makes these windmills turn.

elevator

I like to ride the **elevator** to the top of a building.

enjoy

The children **enjoy** a sunny day at the beach.

A B C D E F G H I J K L M N O P Q R S T U V W X Y Z

enter

We **enter** the school by the front door.

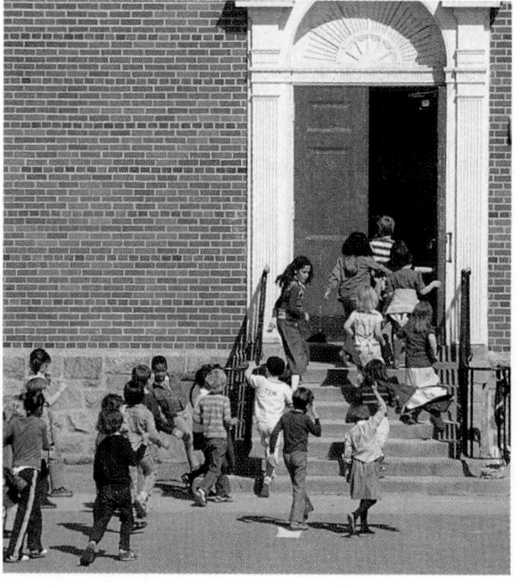

equal

These two crayons are **equal** in length.

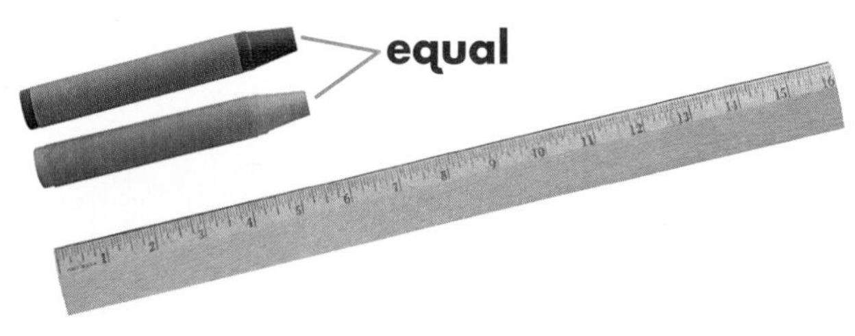

even

The numbers 2, 4, 6, and 8 are **even** numbers.

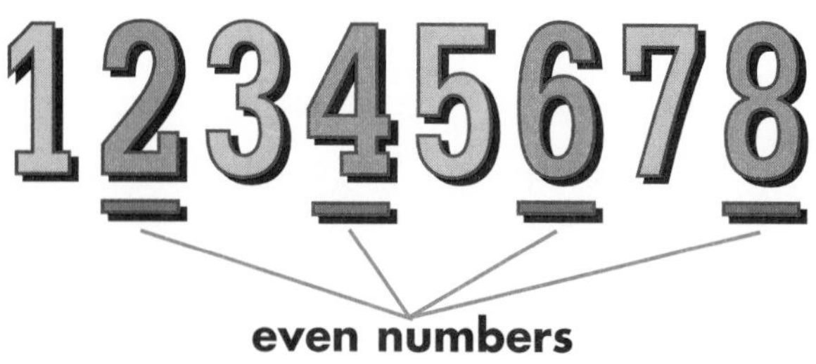

every

Every morning I brush my teeth.

exercise

You can **exercise** in gym class.

exit

We go out through the **exit**.

experiment

Do this **experiment**. Find out what a magnet can pull.

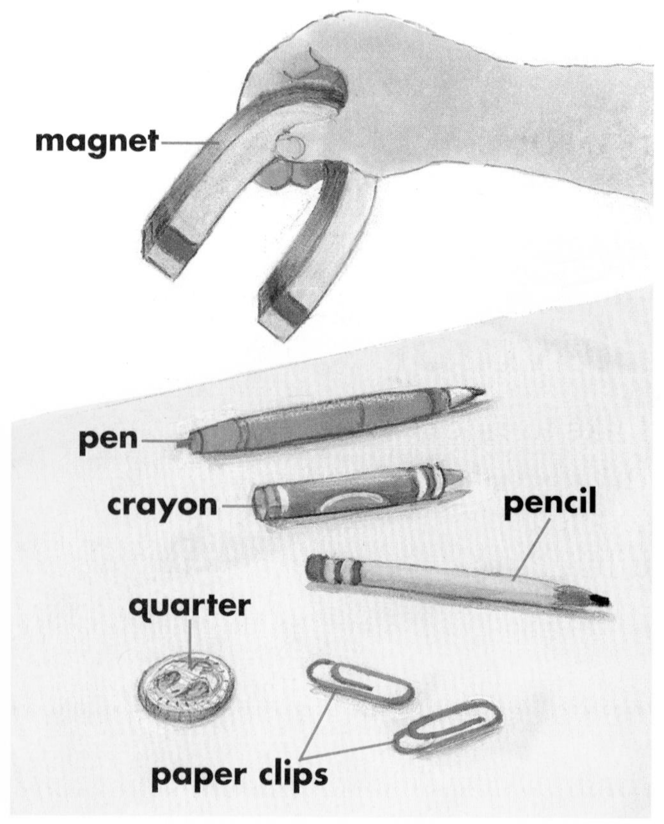

Ff

face

She has a smile on her **face**.

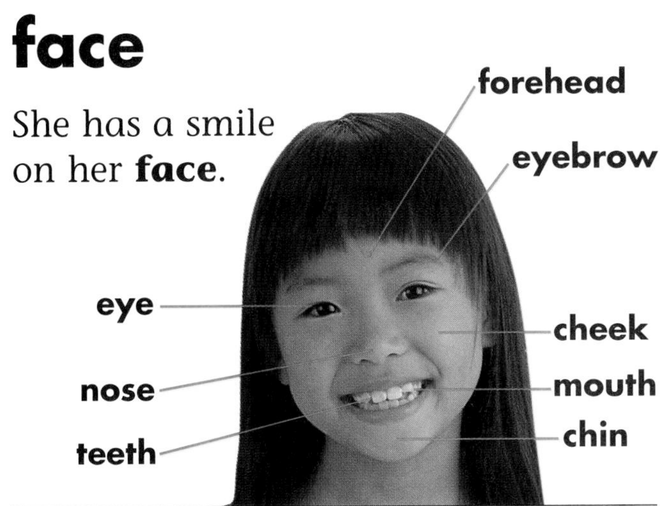

factory

People work with machines in a **factory**. They make products.

Fahrenheit

It's 95° **Fahrenheit**. That's hot!

fair

1. You can have fun at the **fair**.
2. Five for you and none for me? That's not **fair**.

family

There are seven people in this **family**.

a b c d e f g h i j k l m n o p q r s t u v w x y z

Farm Animals

farm

People raise animals and grow crops on a **farm**.

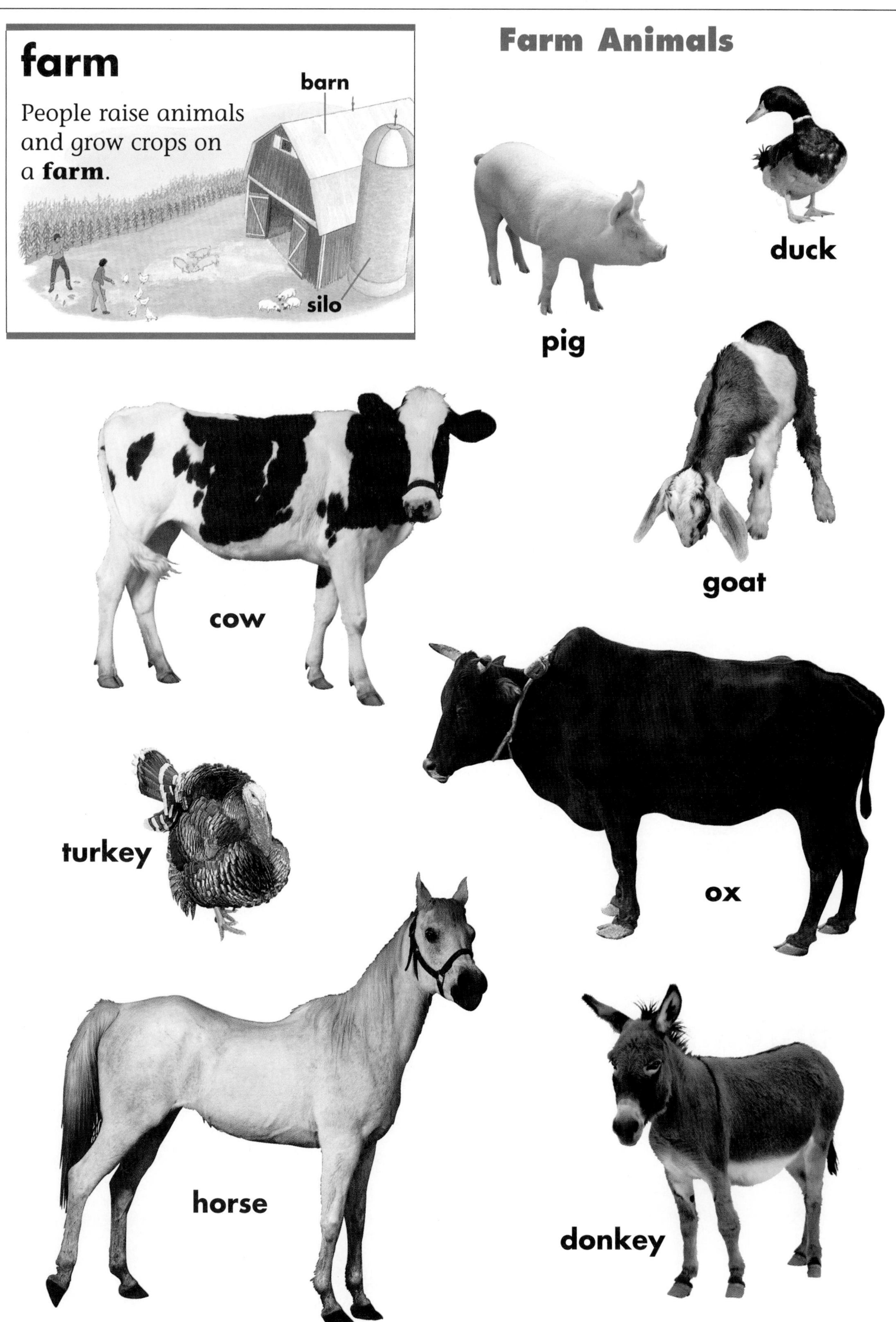

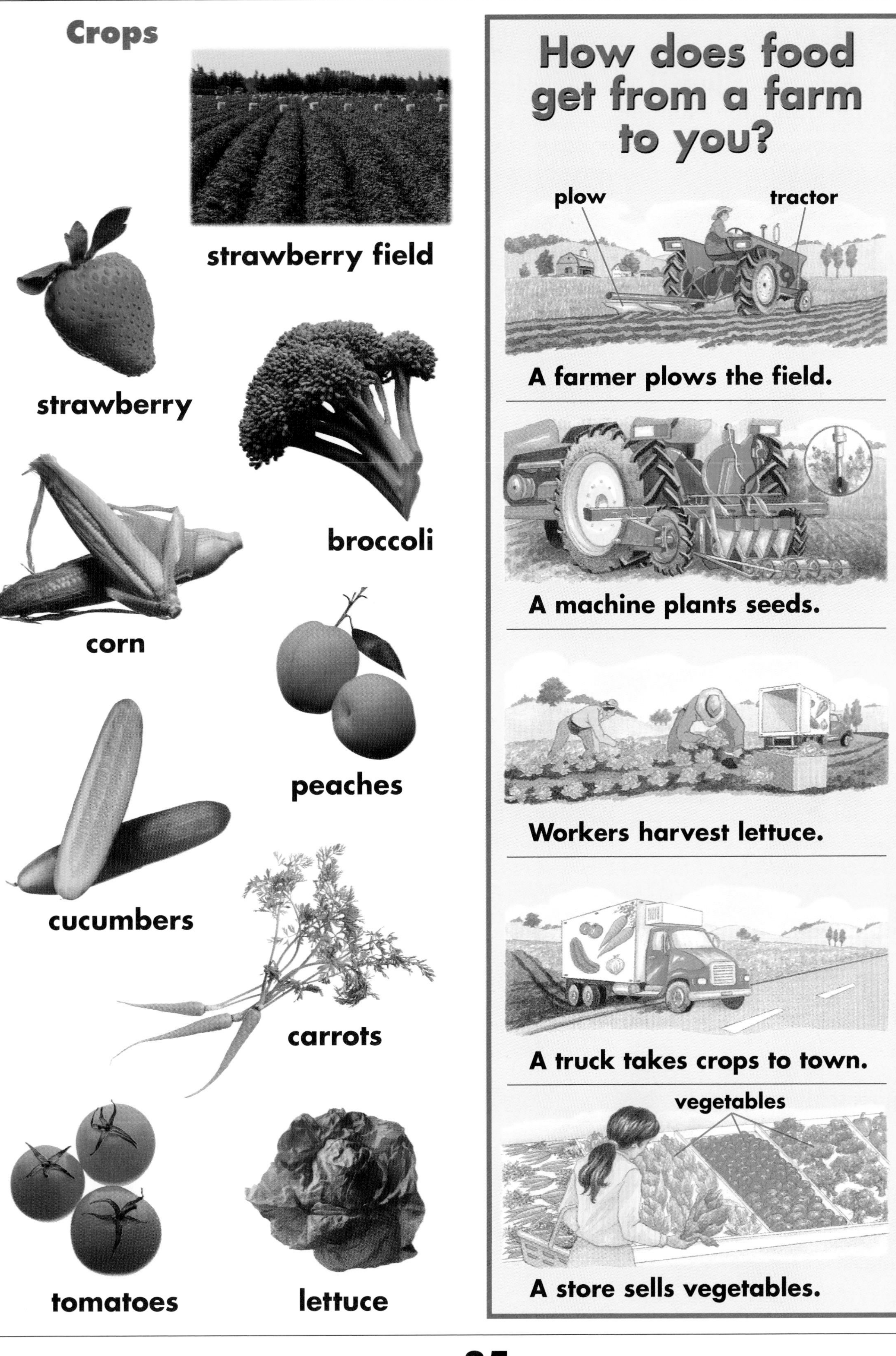

Crops
strawberry field
strawberry
broccoli
corn
peaches
cucumbers
carrots
tomatoes
lettuce
How does food get from a farm to you?
plow
tractor
A farmer plows the field.
A machine plants seeds.
Workers harvest lettuce.
A truck takes crops to town.
vegetables
A store sells vegetables.

A B C D E F G H I J K L M N O P Q R S T U V W X Y Z

feelings

People have **feelings**. They can feel happy or sad, for example.

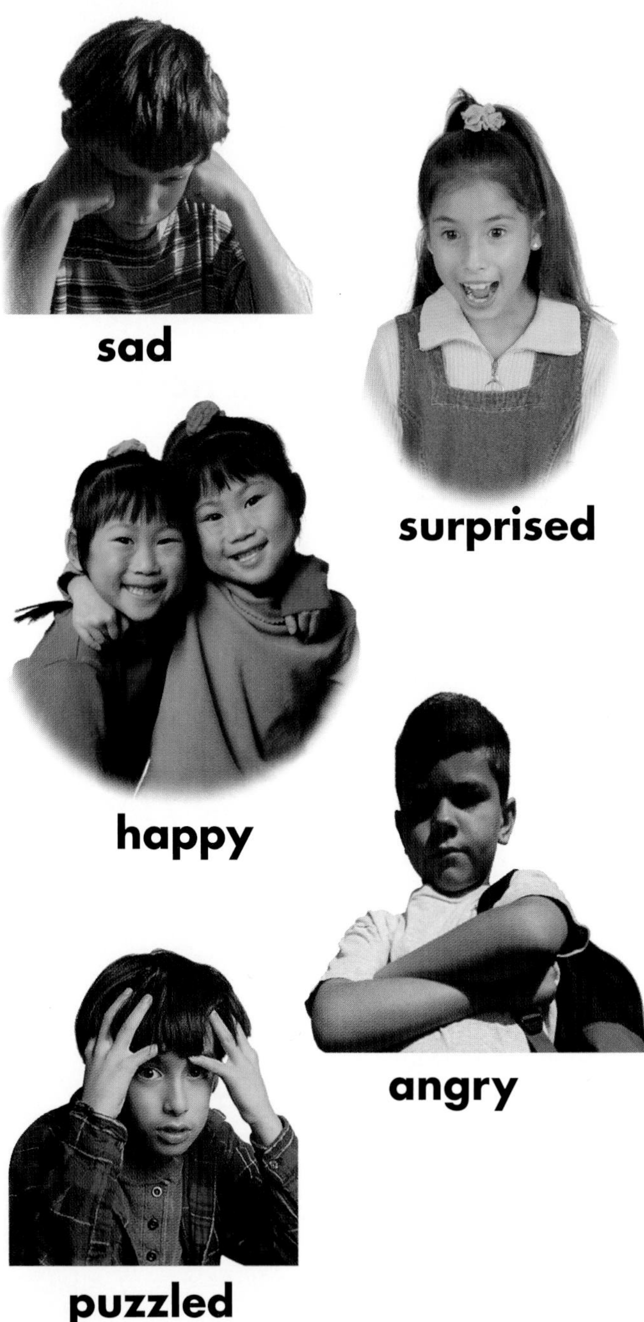

fill

You can **fill** a glass with milk.

find

Nadia lost her book. Where did she **find** it?

finish

She will **finish** her painting soon.

fish

Fish use fins to swim.

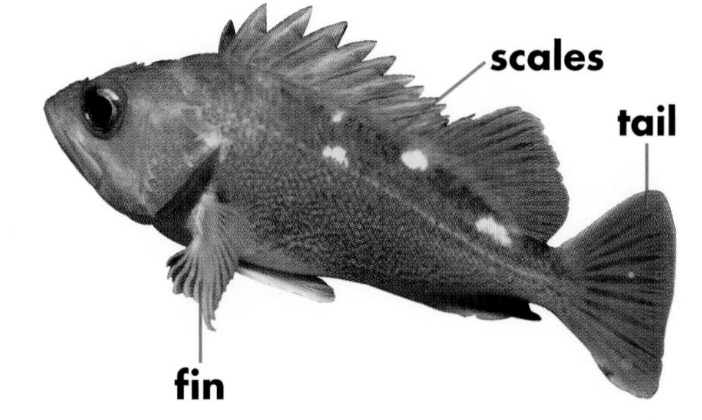

fix

She can **fix** the cup.

flag

The **flag** of the United States has stars and stripes.

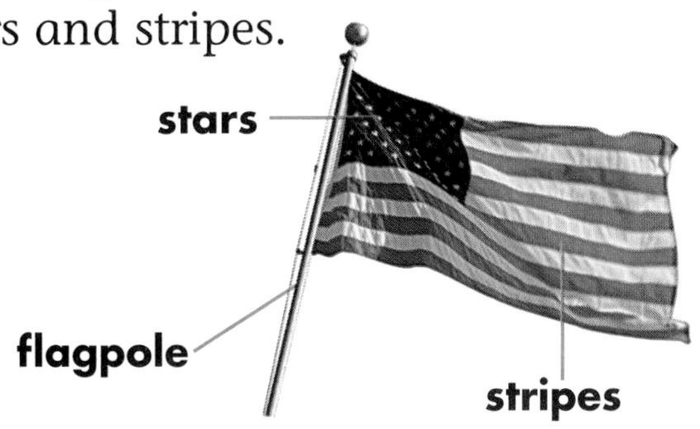

float

These boats can **float** on the water.

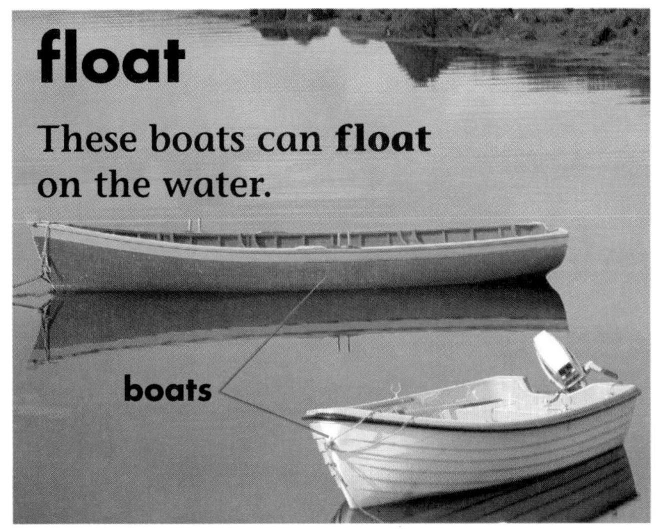

flower

This is my favorite kind of **flower**.

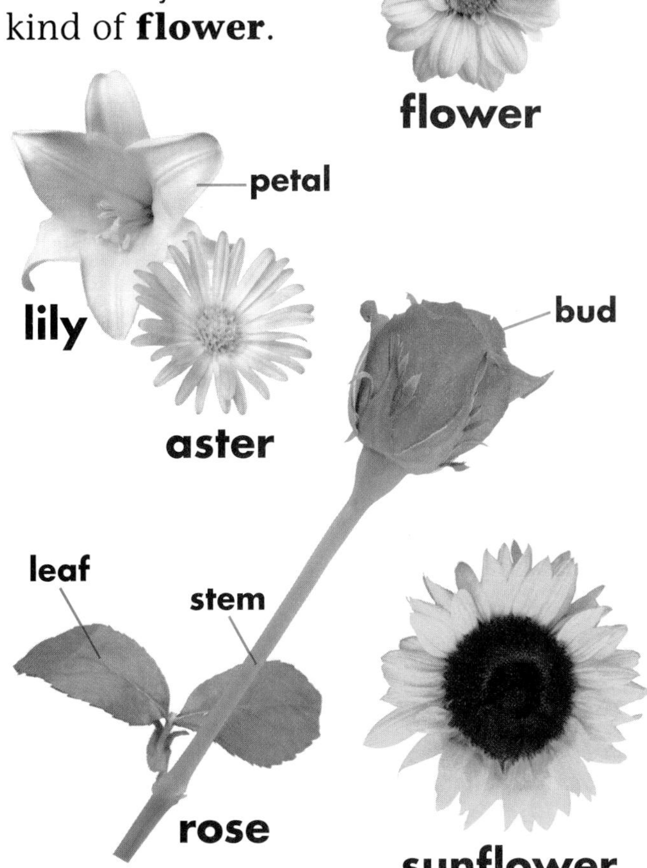

fly

Birds and airplanes can **fly**.

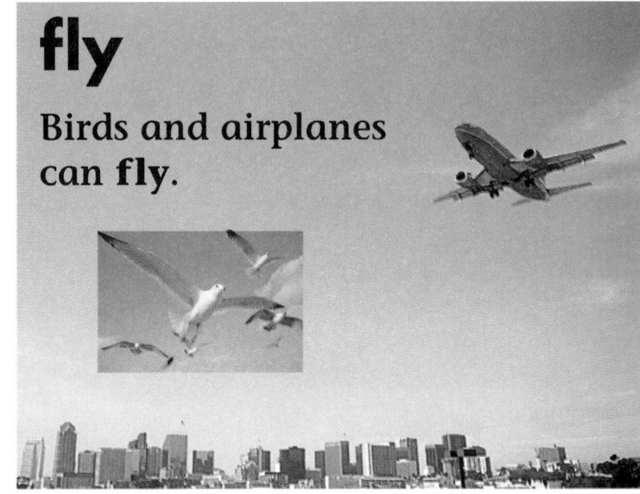

food

There is plenty of **food** to eat.

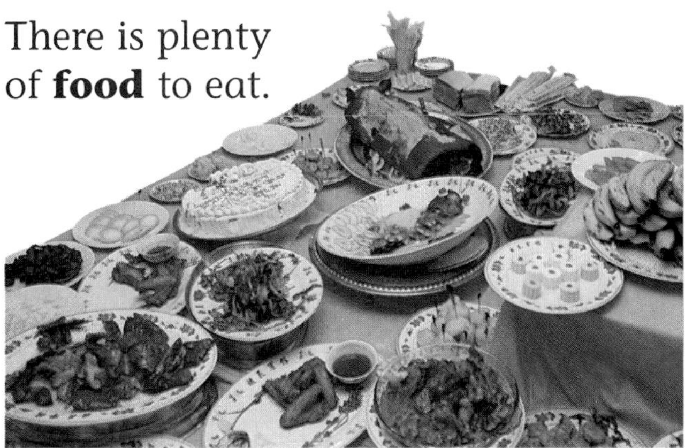

forest

A **forest** has many trees. Lots of animals live in a forest.

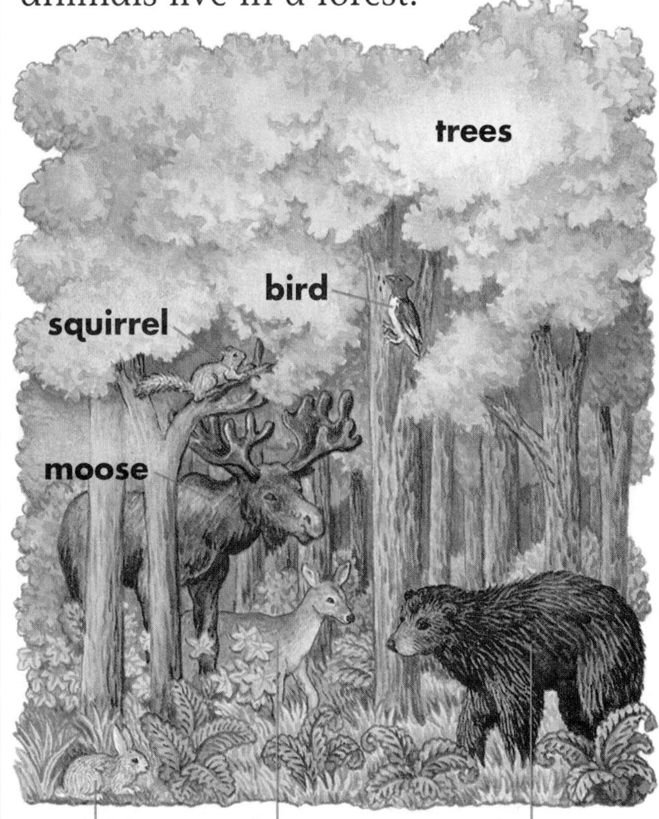

A B C D E F G H I J K L M N O P Q R S T U V W X Y Z

forget

Don't **forget** your lunch!

lunch

forward

She can hop **forward**.

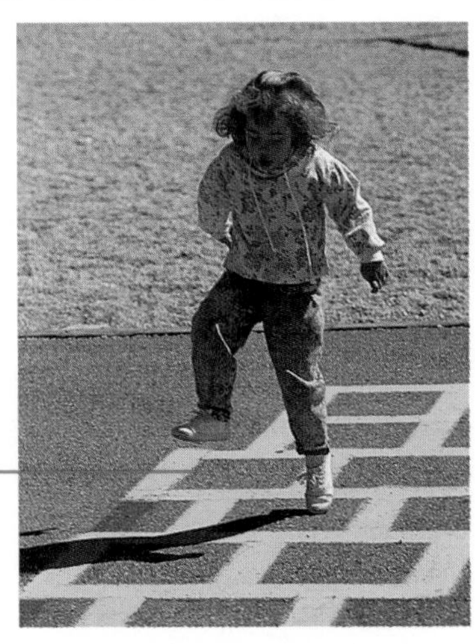

fraction

These **fractions** add up to 1.

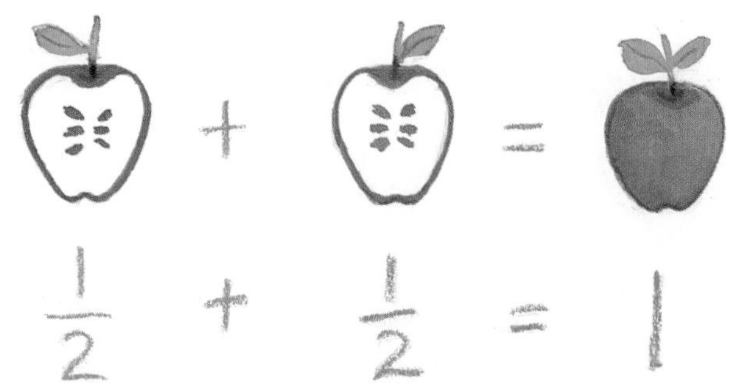

free

She set the bird **free**.

friend

Suzu is Hana's **friend**. Hana is Suzu's friend.

fruit

Fruit is good to eat.

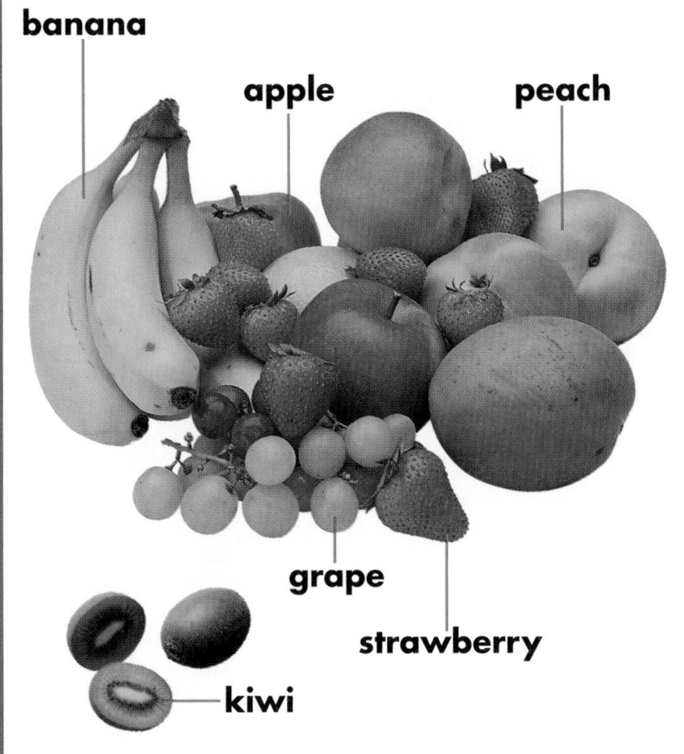

funny

That clown is **funny**! He makes us laugh.

Gg

garbage

He puts the **garbage** in the dumpster.

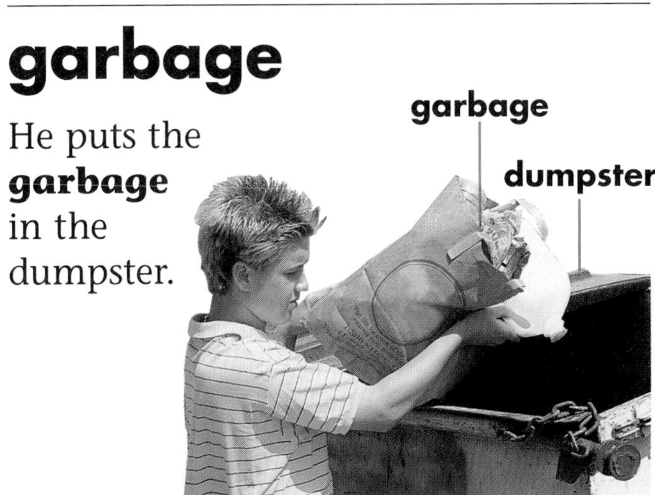

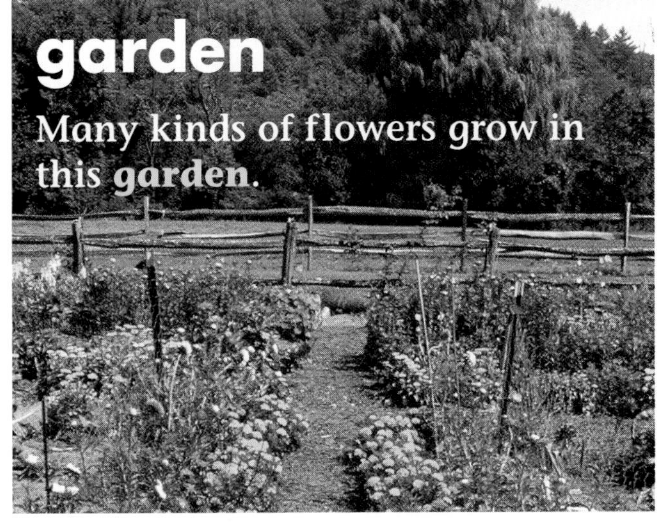

garden

Many kinds of flowers grow in this **garden**.

get

He will **get** his bat.

girl

Vanessa is a **girl**. Linda is a woman.

give

We'll **give** Grandpa a gift.

globe

A **globe** helps us see the shape of the world.

go

We **go** outside to play at recess.

grocery

People buy food in a **grocery** store.

Dairy Foods

Meat

Fruit

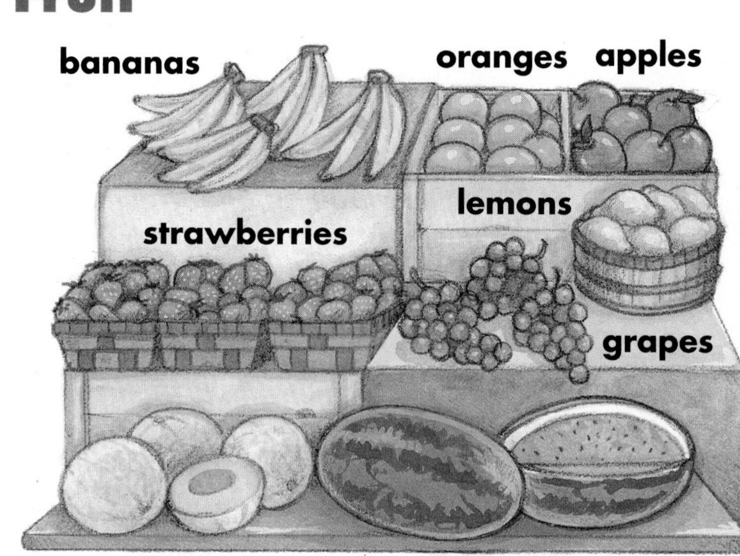

Vegetables

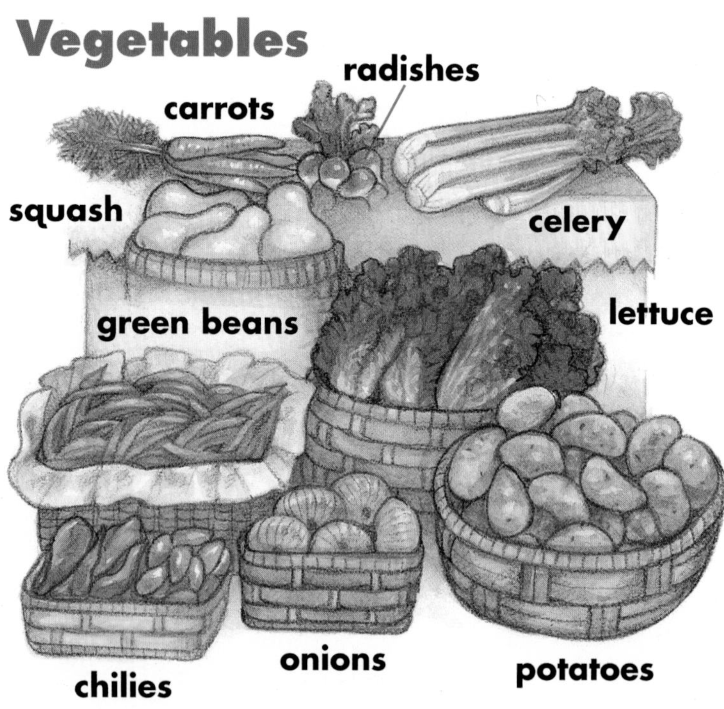

Baked Goods

Packaged Food

Deli Counter

Frozen Foods

Where did these foods come from?

The grapes grew on a farm.

These loaves of bread came from a bakery.

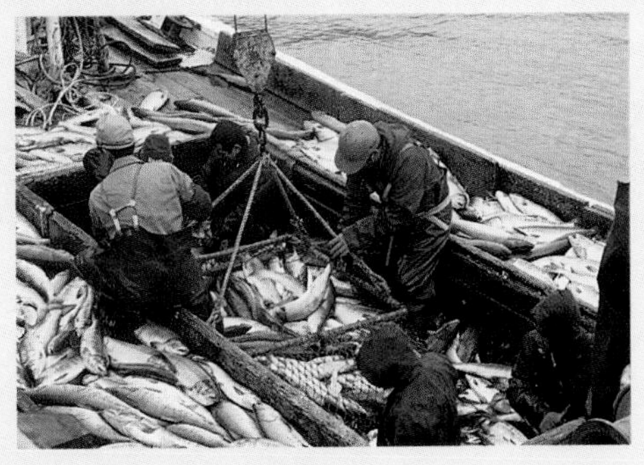

Fishermen caught these fish in the sea.

Workers canned these peas in a cannery.

A B C D E F G H I J K L M N O P Q R S T U V W X Y Z

ground

We plant seeds in the **ground**.

grow

People **grow** and change from year to year.

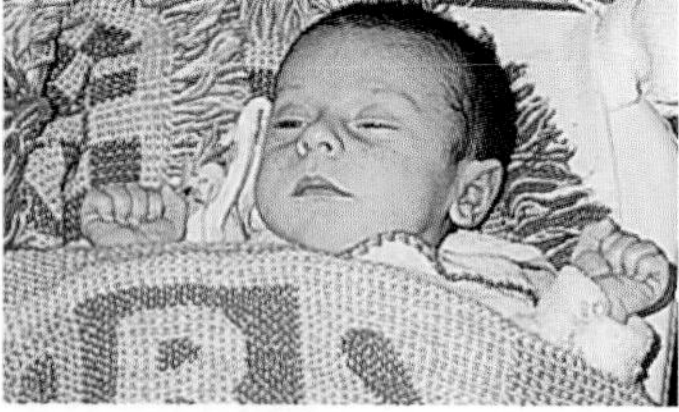

baby

toddler

child

teenager

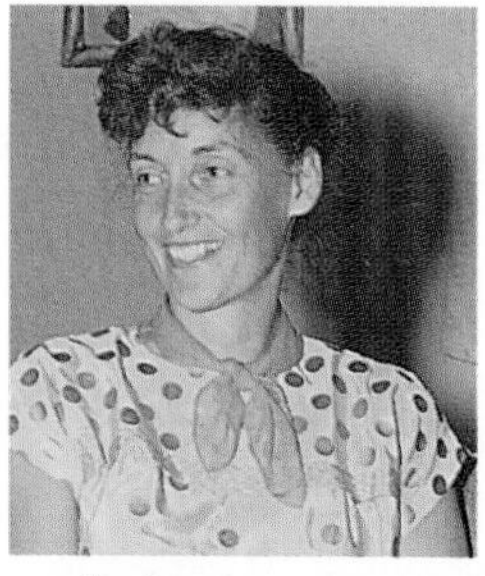

adult

elder

guard

The crossing **guard** helps keep us safe.

guess

Can he **guess** what is in the box?

guide

1. The **guide** tells about the painting.

2. The map will **guide** them.

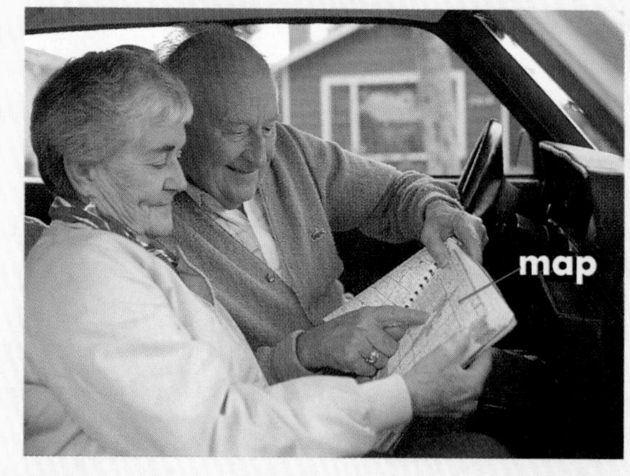

Hh

have

I **have** a new book to read!

half

You may each take **half** of the apple.

heart

This card has a **heart** shape on the front.

harbor

Many boats sail in and out of a **harbor**.

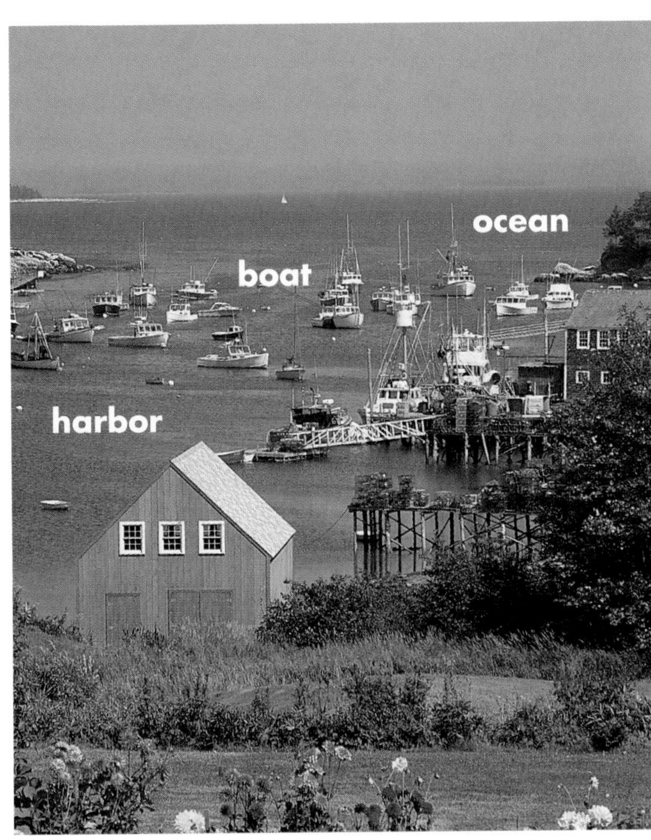

help

The tugboats can **help** the ship come into the harbor.

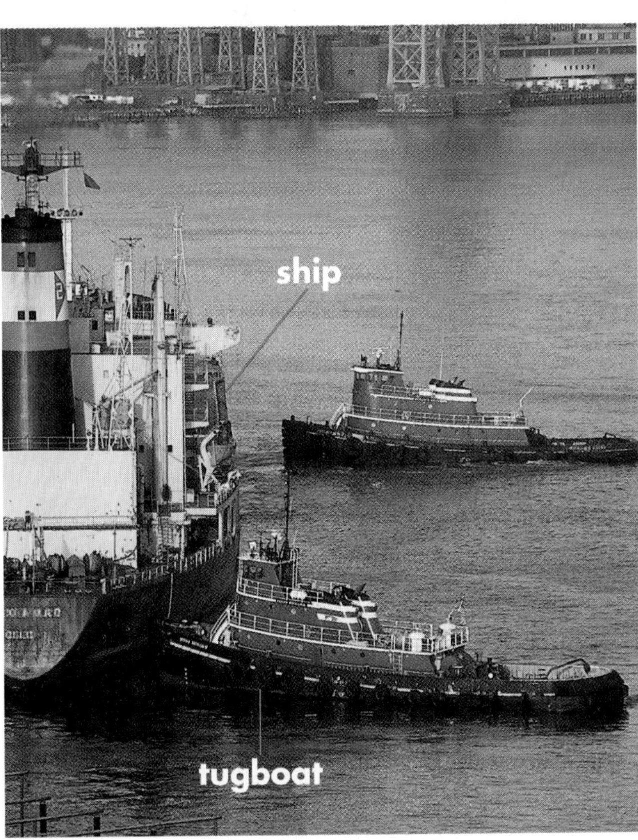

a b c d e f g h i j k l m n o p q r s t u v w x y z

hide

The tiger can **hide** in the grass.

hill

The fence goes over the **hill**.

hold

The baby can **hold** a bottle.

holiday

Thanksgiving is a special day. It is a **holiday**.

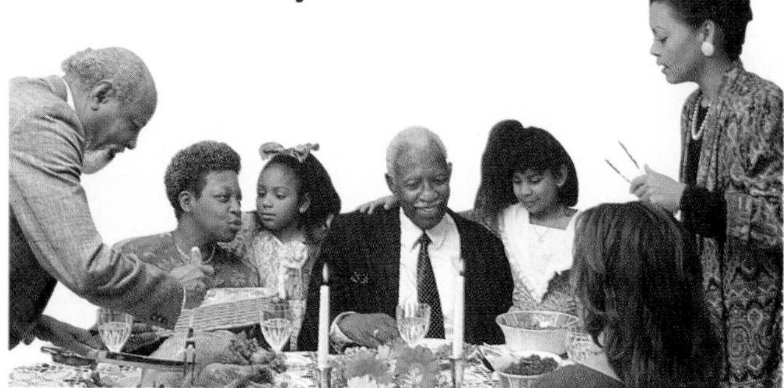

home

What kind of **home** do you live in?

city apartments

cottage

log cabin

bamboo house

houseboat

adobe home

a b c d e f g h i j k l m n o p q r s t u v w x y z

A B C D E F G H I J K L M N O P Q R S T U V W X Y Z

howl

A coyote may **howl** at the moon.

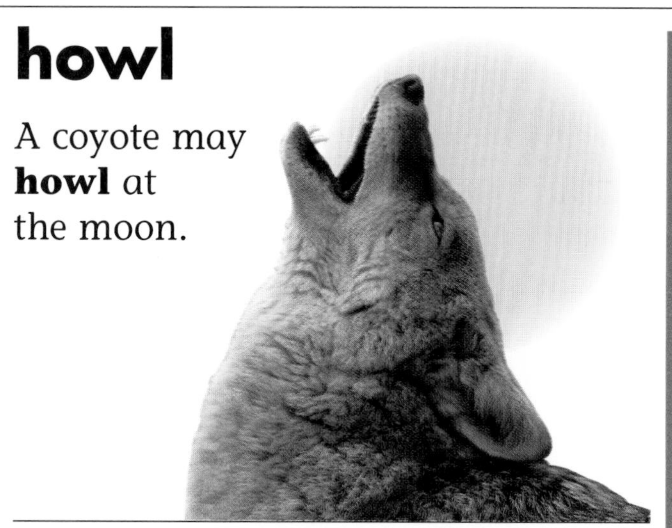

hug

I like to **hug** my teddy bear.

huge

This is a **huge** tree.

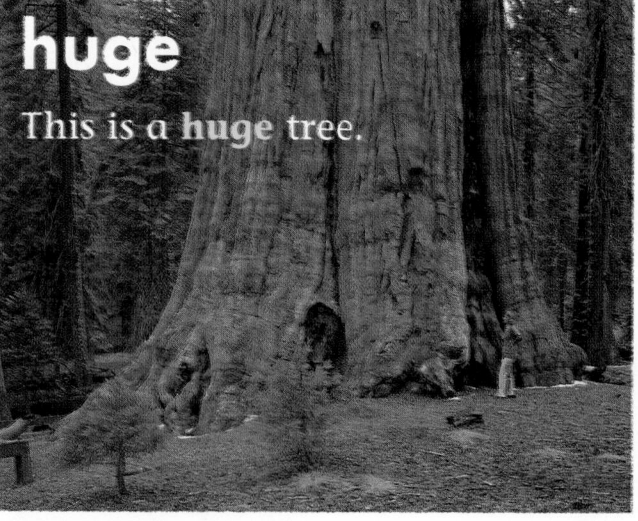

hungry

Is it time to eat? I'm **hungry**!

hunt

A hawk can **hunt** for food from the air.

hurry

We have to **hurry** to catch the bus!

hurt

Ouch! I **hurt** my knee!

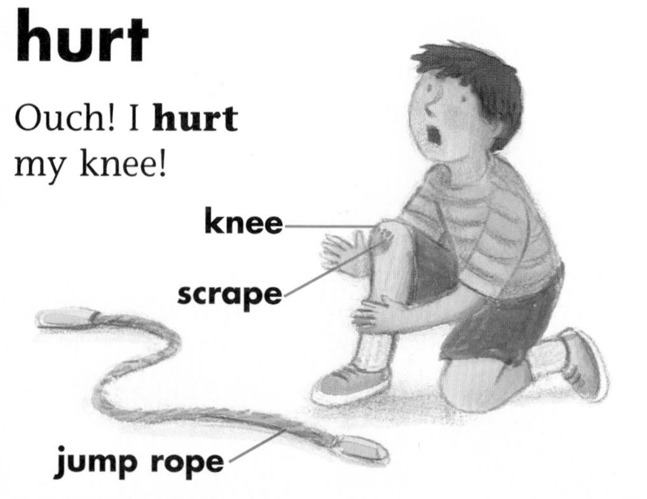

husband

Mr. Davis is the **husband** of Mrs. Davis.

Ii

ice

You can skate on **ice**.

idea

What a good **idea**!

ill

Geena is **ill** today.

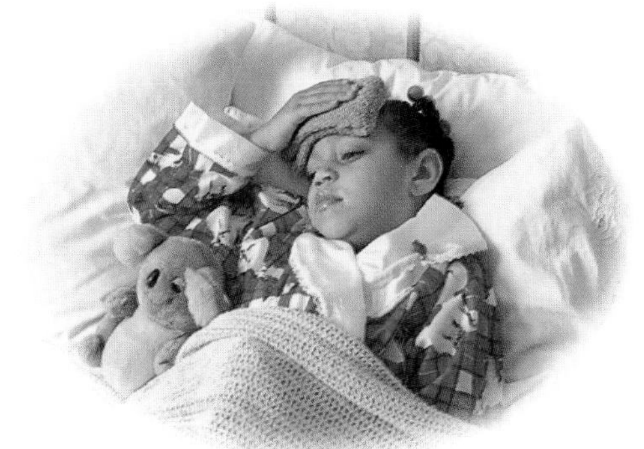

imagine

It is fun to **imagine** things.

include

The teacher will **include** everyone in the activity.

information

You can find **information** in many places.

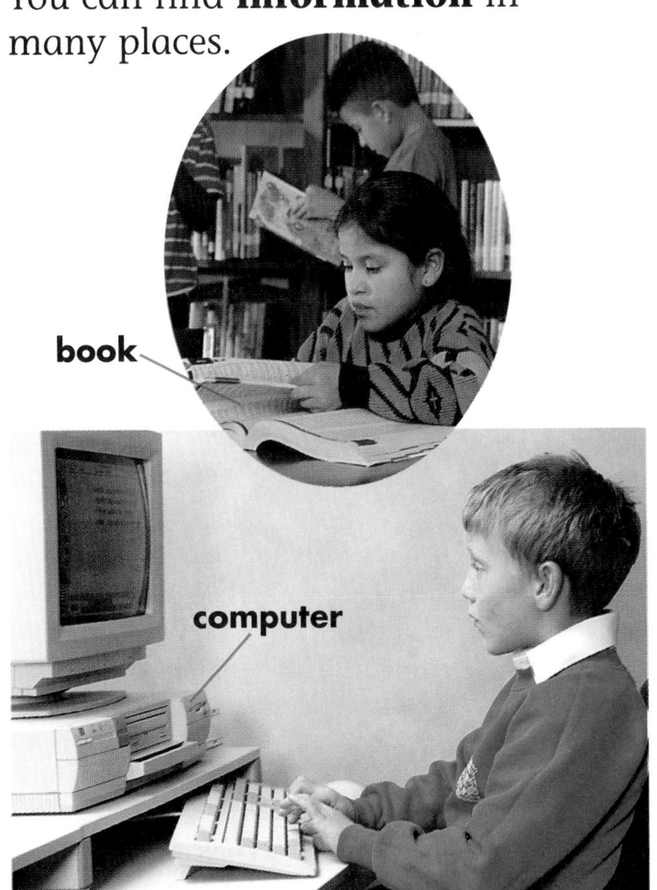

A B C D E F G H I J K L M N O P Q R S T U V W X Y Z

insect

An **insect** always has six legs.

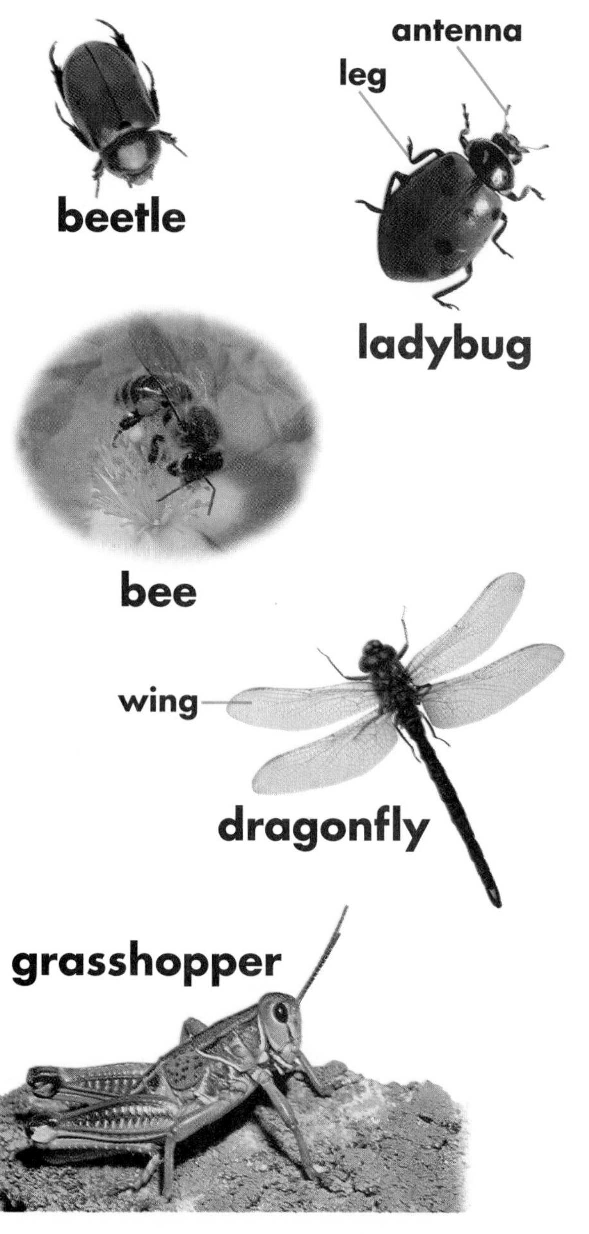

Butterfly Life Cycle

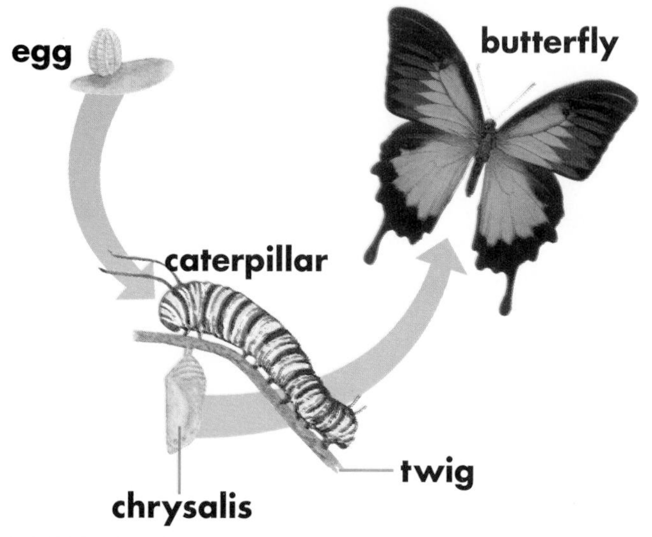

interesting

This is an **interesting** book. I like it a lot.

international

These are **international** flags. They come from many countries.

invitation

This is an **invitation** to parents.

Please come to our class art show.
Date: Thursday, March 5
Time: 3:00 p.m.
Place: Room 20

island

Puerto Rico is an **island**.

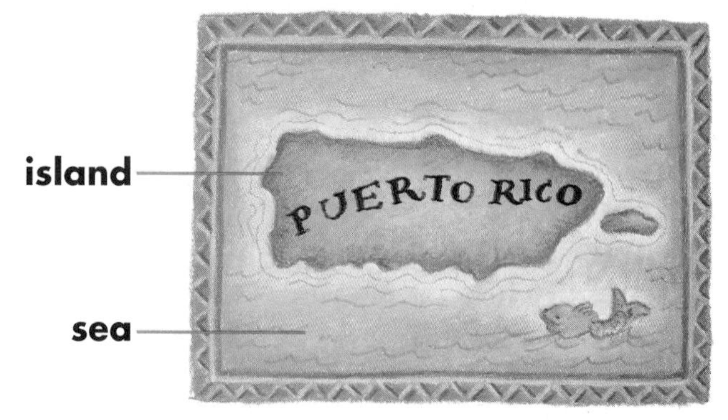

Jj

journey

It is a long **journey** to the lake.

jar

This **jar** has pennies in it.

lid
jar
pennies

judge

The **judge** will listen to both sides of the story.

job

My **job** is to walk the dog. Tim's job is to set the table.

juice

You can make **juice** from oranges.

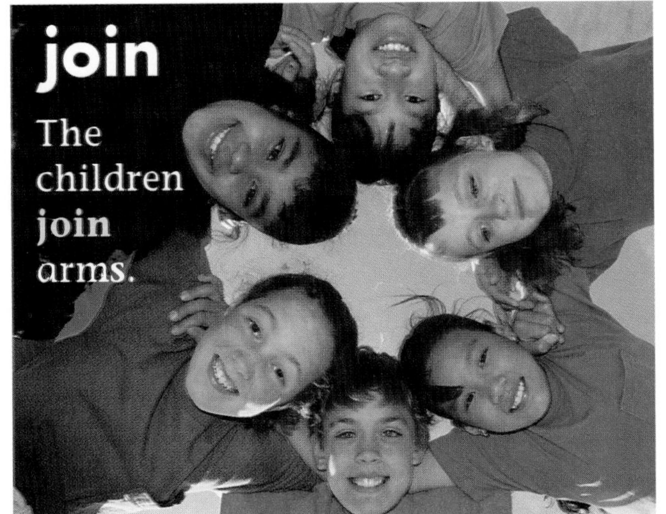

jump

I can **jump** up in the air.

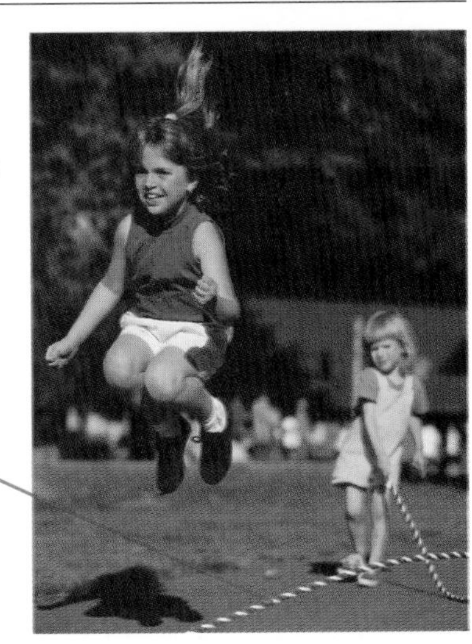

jungle

In the **jungle**
it is warm.
It rains a lot.
Many plants
and animals
live in the
jungle.

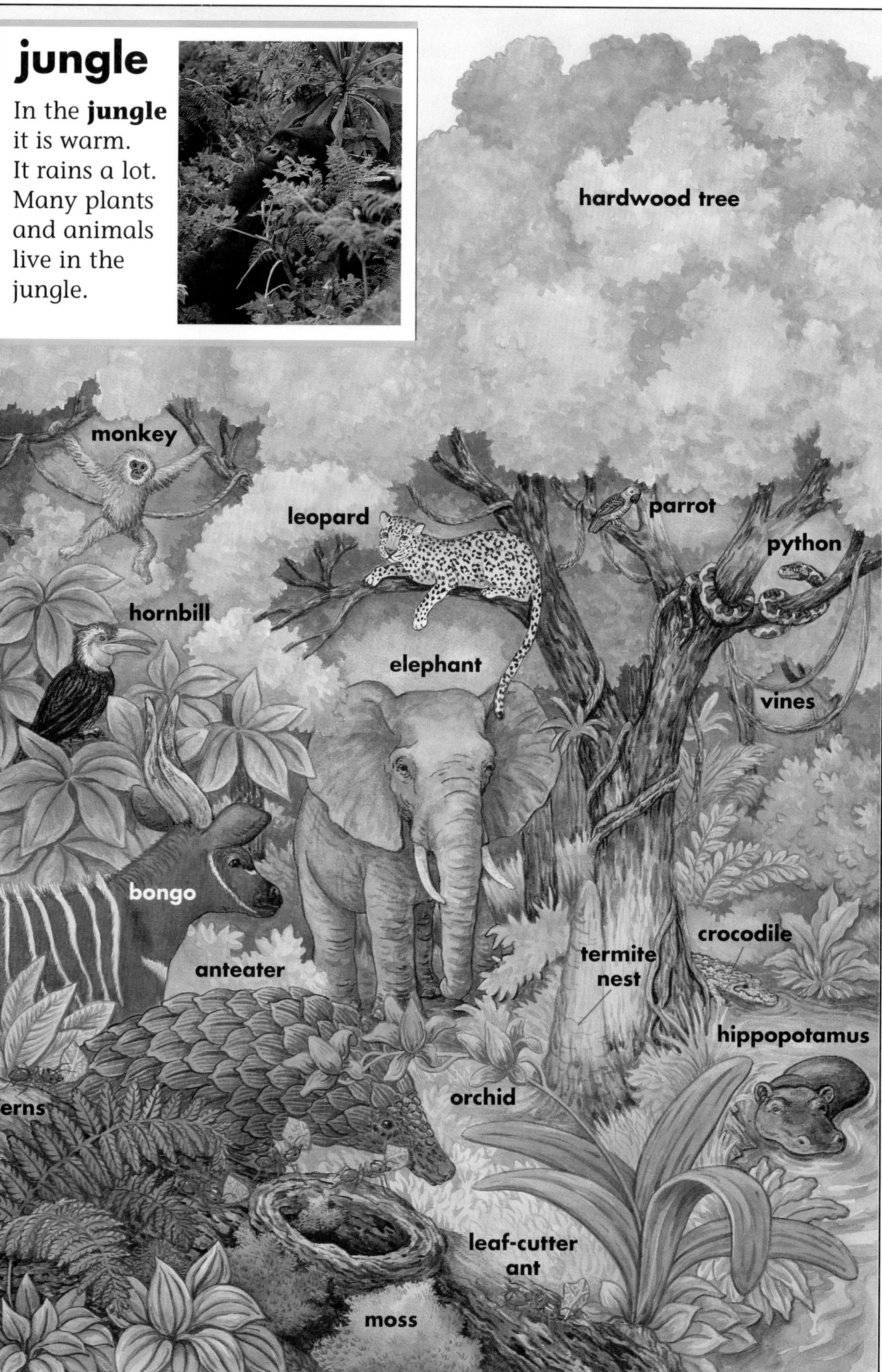

Kk

keep

You can **keep** your work in a folder.

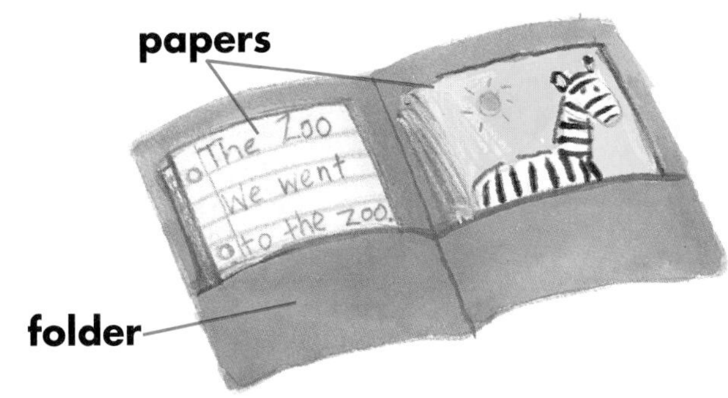

key

❶ You can use a **key** to open a lock.

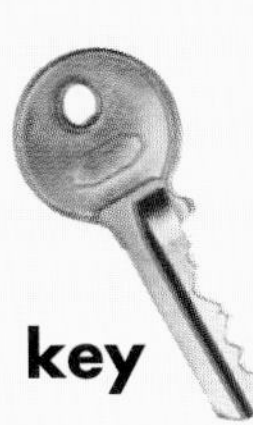

❷ You touch a computer **key** to type a letter.

kick

You **kick** a ball with your foot.

kind

❶ What **kind** of fruit do you want?

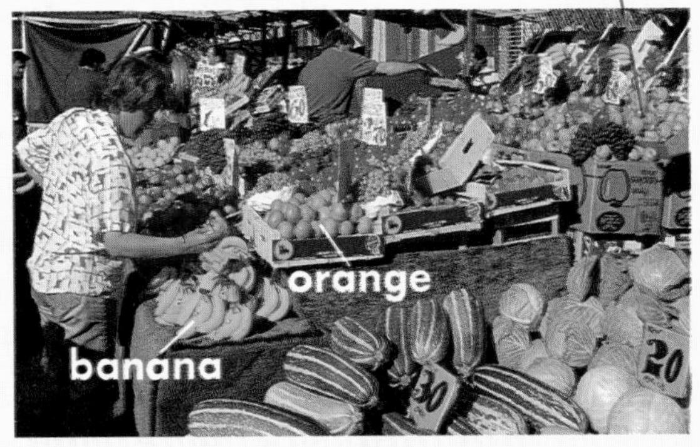

❷ This is a **kind** thing to do.

kiss

This mother loves to **kiss** her baby!

kitchen

You cook food in a **kitchen**.

kite

It is fun to fly a **kite** on a windy day.

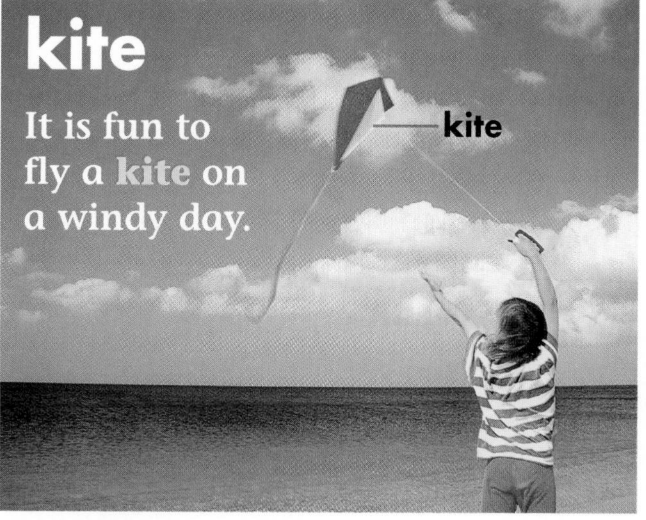

knife

A cook uses a **knife** to cut food.

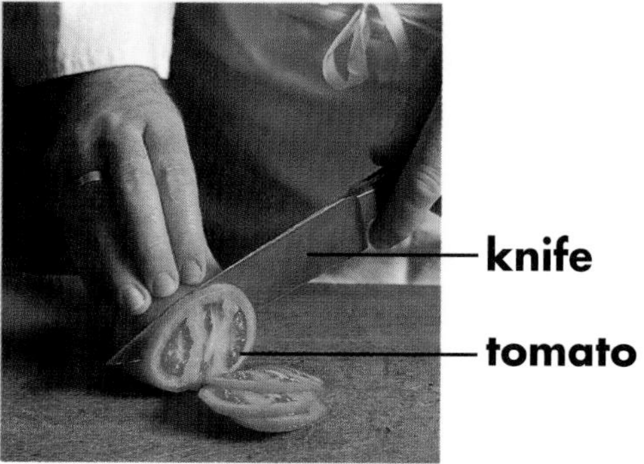

knight

This book is about a **knight** and his horse.

knock

Always **knock** before you open a door.

knot

You can tie a **knot** with a piece of string.

know

I **know** how to ride a bike now!

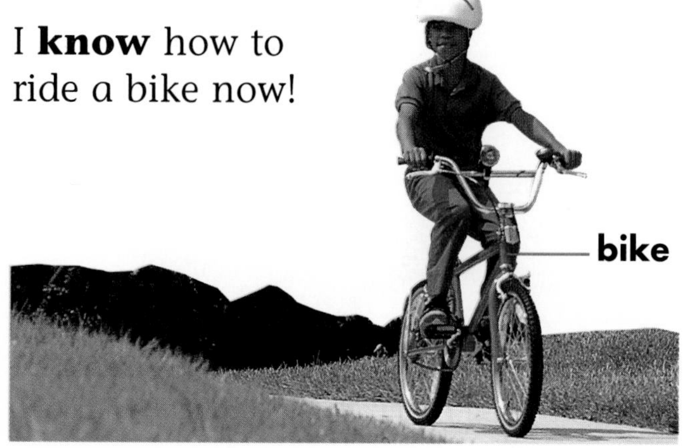

A B C D E F G H I J K L M N O P Q R S T U V W X Y Z

Ll

lake

It is quiet on the **lake**.

land

① The lake has **land** all around it.

② The plane will **land** at the airport.

language

You use your hands to speak sign **language**.

last

December is the **last** month in the year.

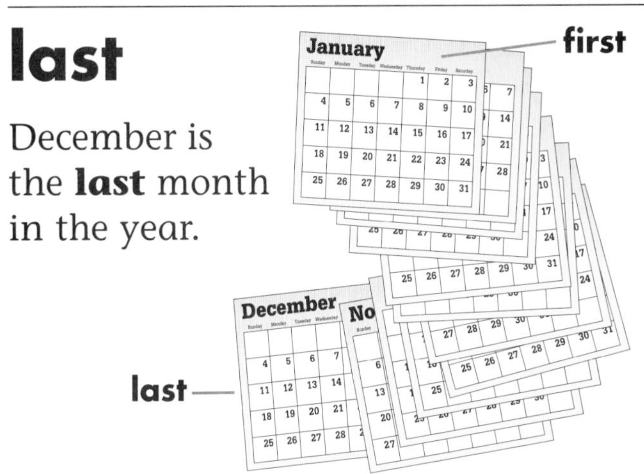

late

Oh, no! Nick is **late** for the school bus.

laugh

Friends love to **laugh** together.

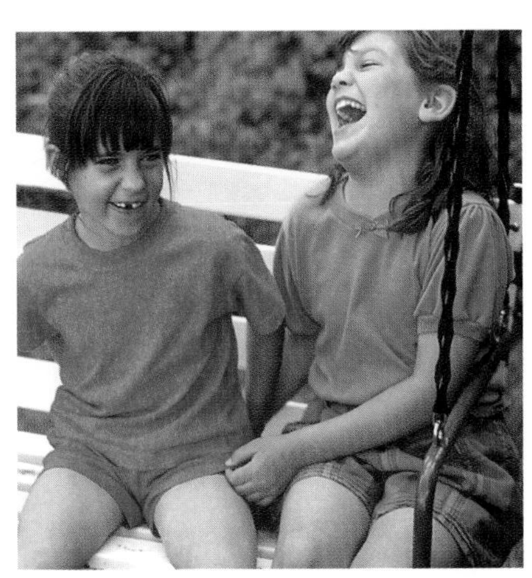

learn

You can **learn** how to dive at a pool.

leave

We **leave** home at 8 o'clock in the morning.

left

He is raising his **left** hand.

left hand

less

Fran has **less** cake than Carlos. Matt has the least cake.

lesson

Mike has a piano **lesson** each week. He wants to play well.

teacher

piano

student

letter

1. The **letter** Z is the last letter in this alphabet.

A B C D E F G H I
J K L M N O P Q R
S T U V W X Y Z

2. Juan is reading a **letter** from his grandmother.

library

You can borrow books from a **library**.

books

lift

Bend your legs when you **lift** something heavy.

live

Lisa and Kenny Brown **live** at 28 Clark Road.

light

Nico turns on the **light** to read.

living room

You can read, talk, or watch television in the **living room**.

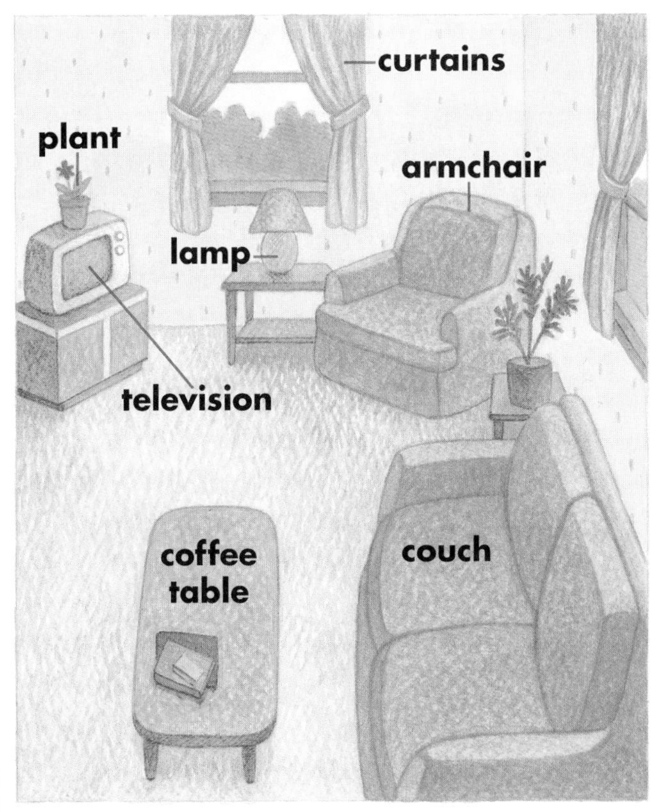

line

You can draw a straight **line** or a curved one.

straight line

curved line

litter

Let's clean up this **litter**.

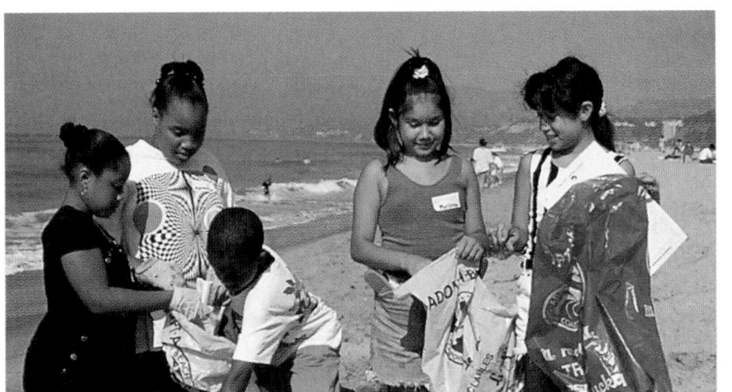

lunch

I like to eat **lunch** with my friend.

a b c d e f g h i j k **l** m n o p q r s t u v w x y z

A
B
C
D
E
F
G
H
I
J
K
L
M
N
O
P
Q
R
S
T
U
V
W
X
Y
Z

Mm

machine

A **machine** has many parts. People use machines to help do work.

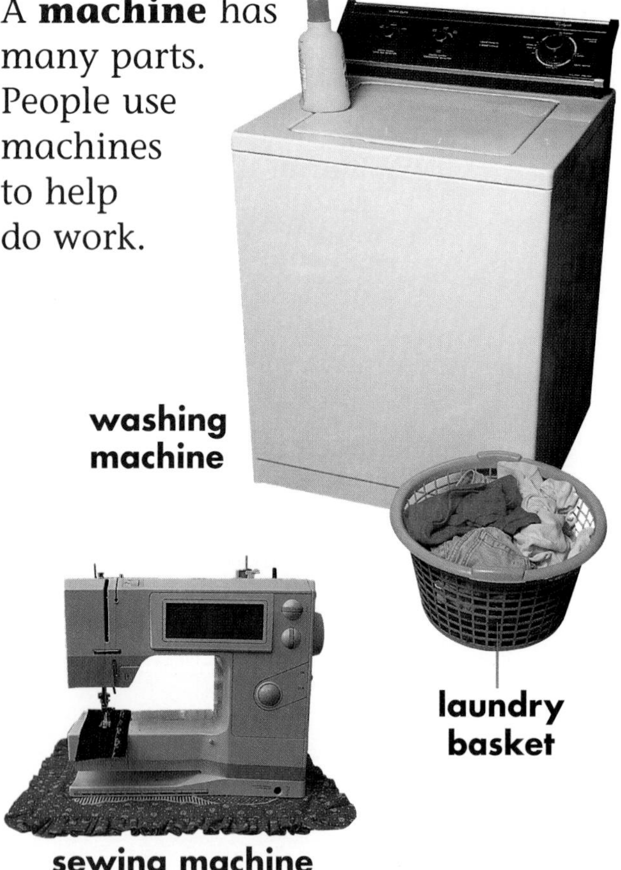

magnet

A **magnet** can pull a paper clip.

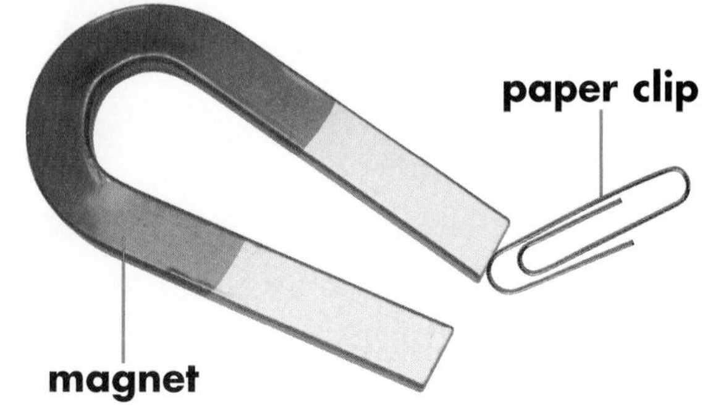

mail

Amy will **mail** a letter.

mailbox

Amy puts her letter in the **mailbox**.

main

Goldilocks is one of the **main** characters in this story.

make

He will **make** a house out of blocks.

make-believe

Fairy tales are **make-believe** stories. They are not real.

mammal

A **mammal** feeds milk to its babies. All these animals are mammals.

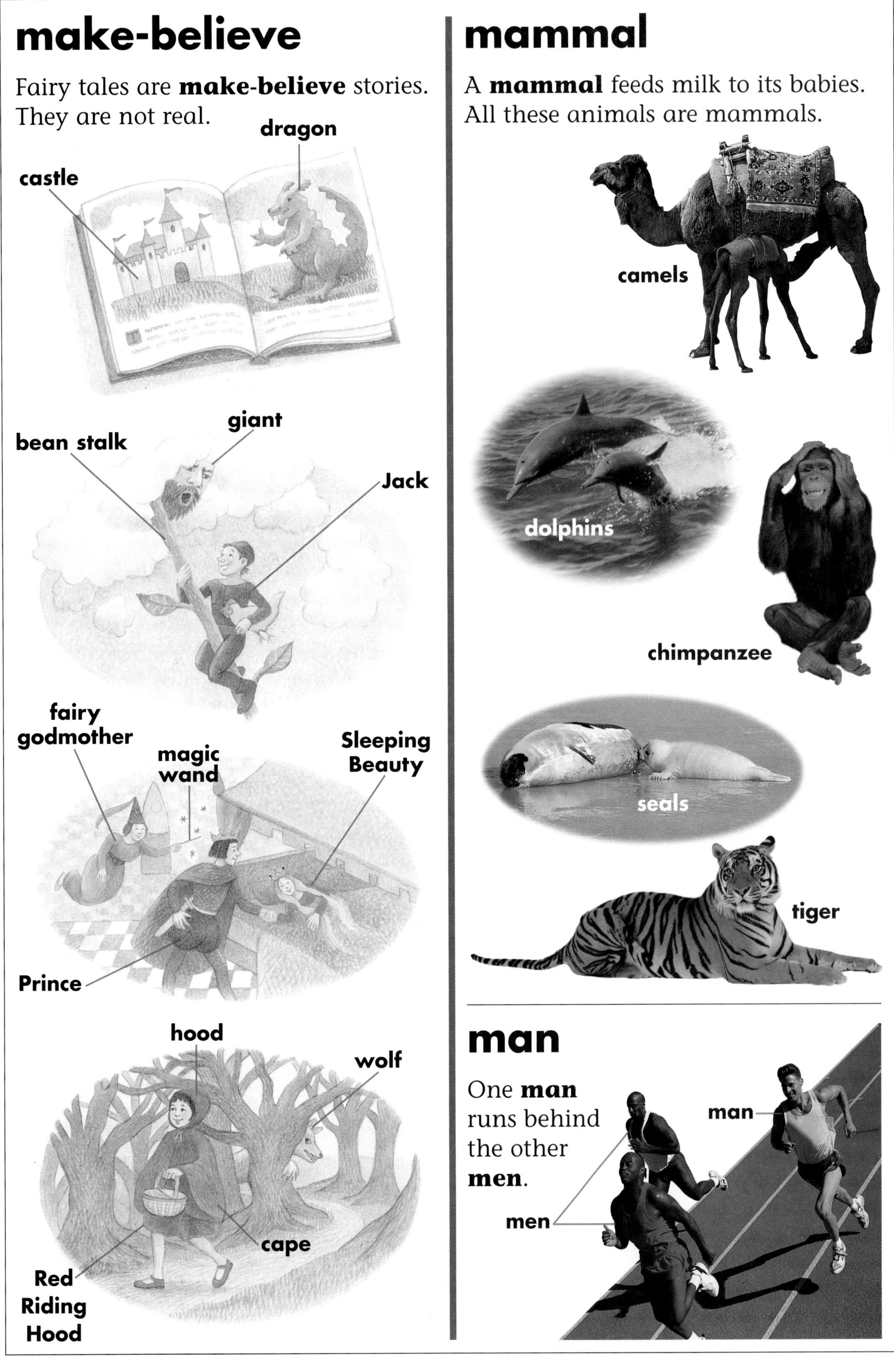

man

One **man** runs behind the other **men**.

a b c d e f g h i j k l m n o p q r s t u v w x y z

A
B
C
D
E
F
G
H
I
J
K
L
M
N
O
P
Q
R
S
T
U
V
W
X
Y
Z

map

A **map** can help you learn about a place.

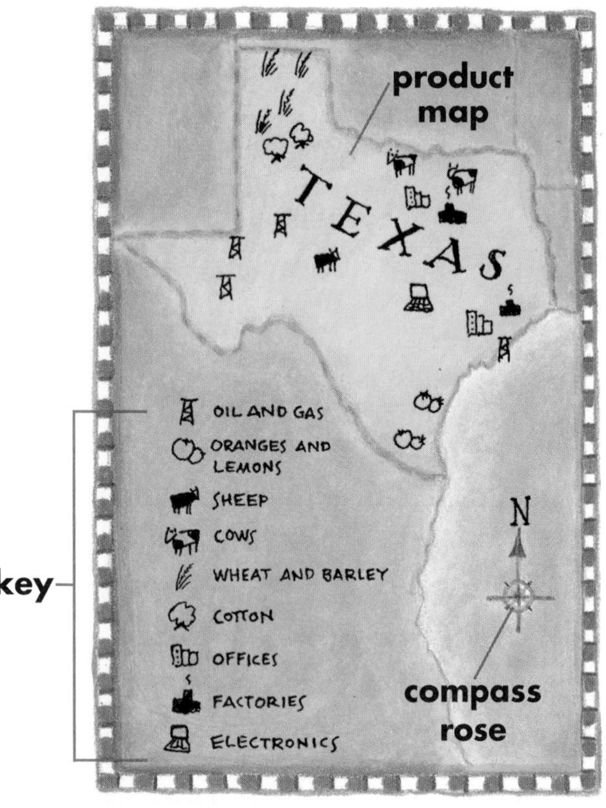

march

This band can **march** in a parade.

market

This **market** is a great place to buy fruits and vegetables.

marry

At a wedding, a man and a woman **marry** each other.

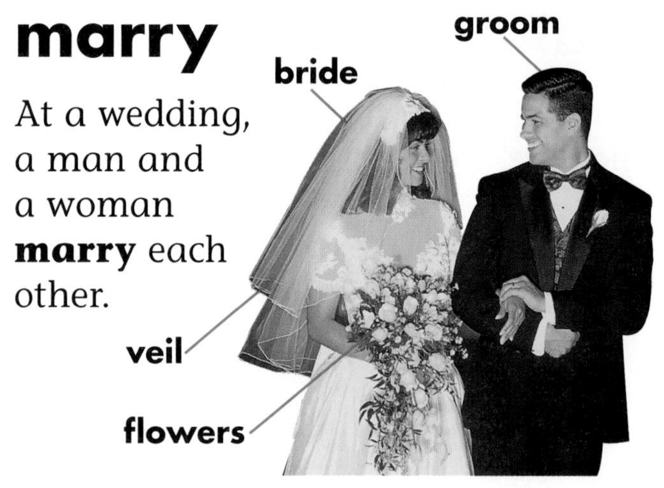

mask

You can wear a **mask** to cover your face.

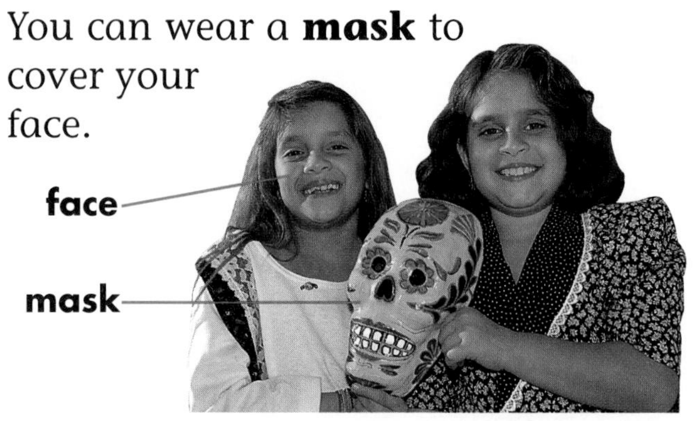

match

These two socks **match**. They are a pair.

maybe

Maybe it will rain. I guess I should take my umbrella.

measure

You can **measure** things with a ruler.

ruler

Measuring Height and Weight

scale

Measuring Length

ruler

tape measure

Measuring Volume

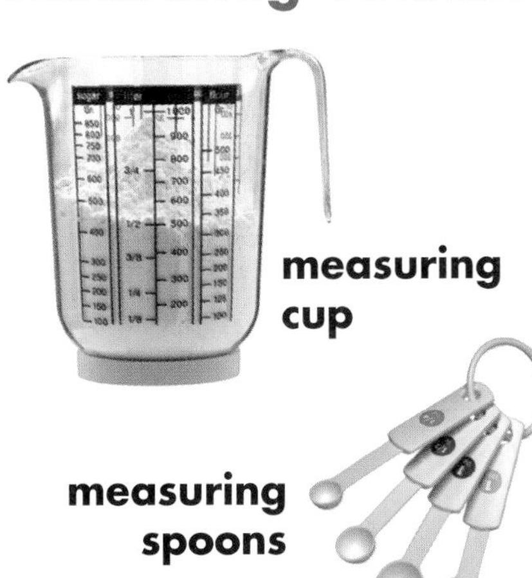

measuring cup

measuring spoons

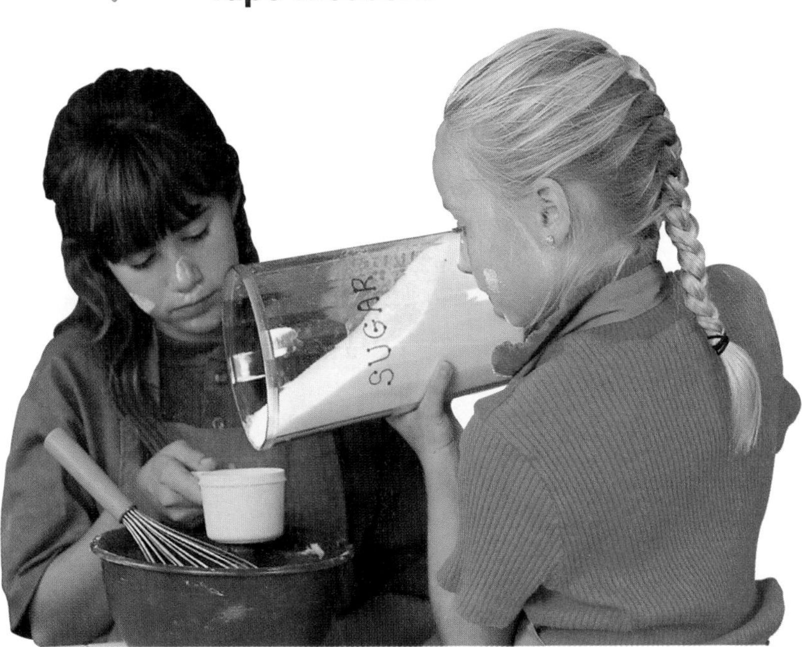

A B C D E F G H I J K L M N O P Q R S T U V W X Y Z

middle

The monkey is in the **middle.**

money

You can buy things with **money**.

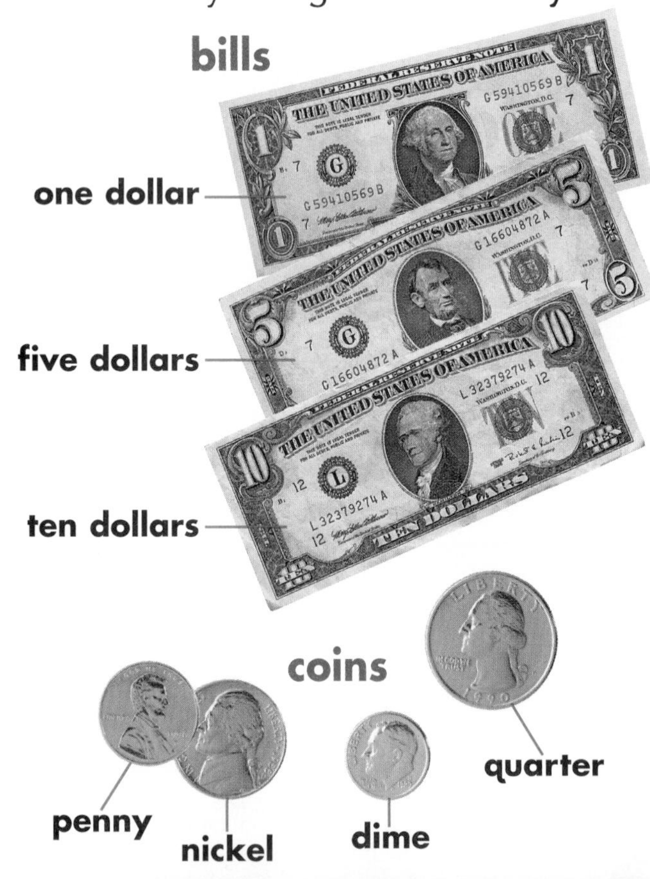

moon

The **moon** is full tonight.

more

Rob has **more** books than Jana. Lisa has the most books.

morning

Isabel wakes up early in the **morning**.

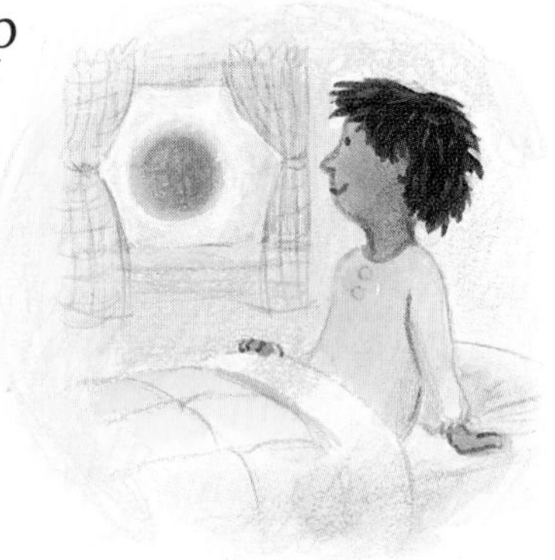

mountain

A **mountain** may be covered with snow in the summer.

music

This boy plays **music** on the piano.

Nn

name

The **name** of my dog is Fluffy.

narrow

The tube is very **narrow**. The hamster will not fit.

nation

This **nation** is called Mexico.

nature

Rocks, plants, and animals are all part of **nature**.

necessary

Water is **necessary** for plants to live.

need

Babies **need** milk to grow.

neighbor

We help our **neighbor** rake the leaves.

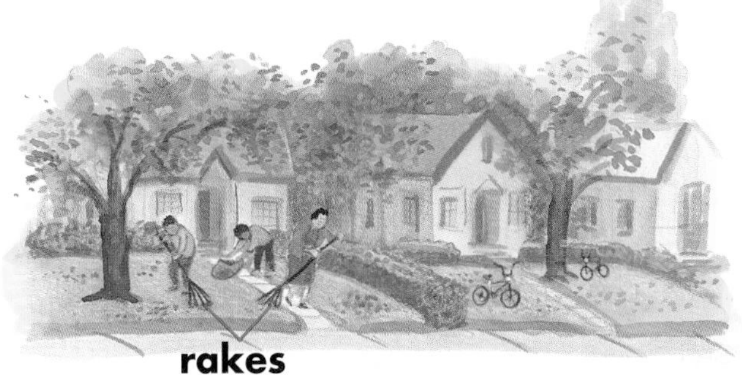

a b c d e f g h i j k l m n o p q r s t u v w x y z

A
B
C
D
E
F
G
H
I
J
K
L
M
N
O
P
Q
R
S
T
U
V
W
X
Y
Z

neighborhood

People live and work in a **neighborhood**.

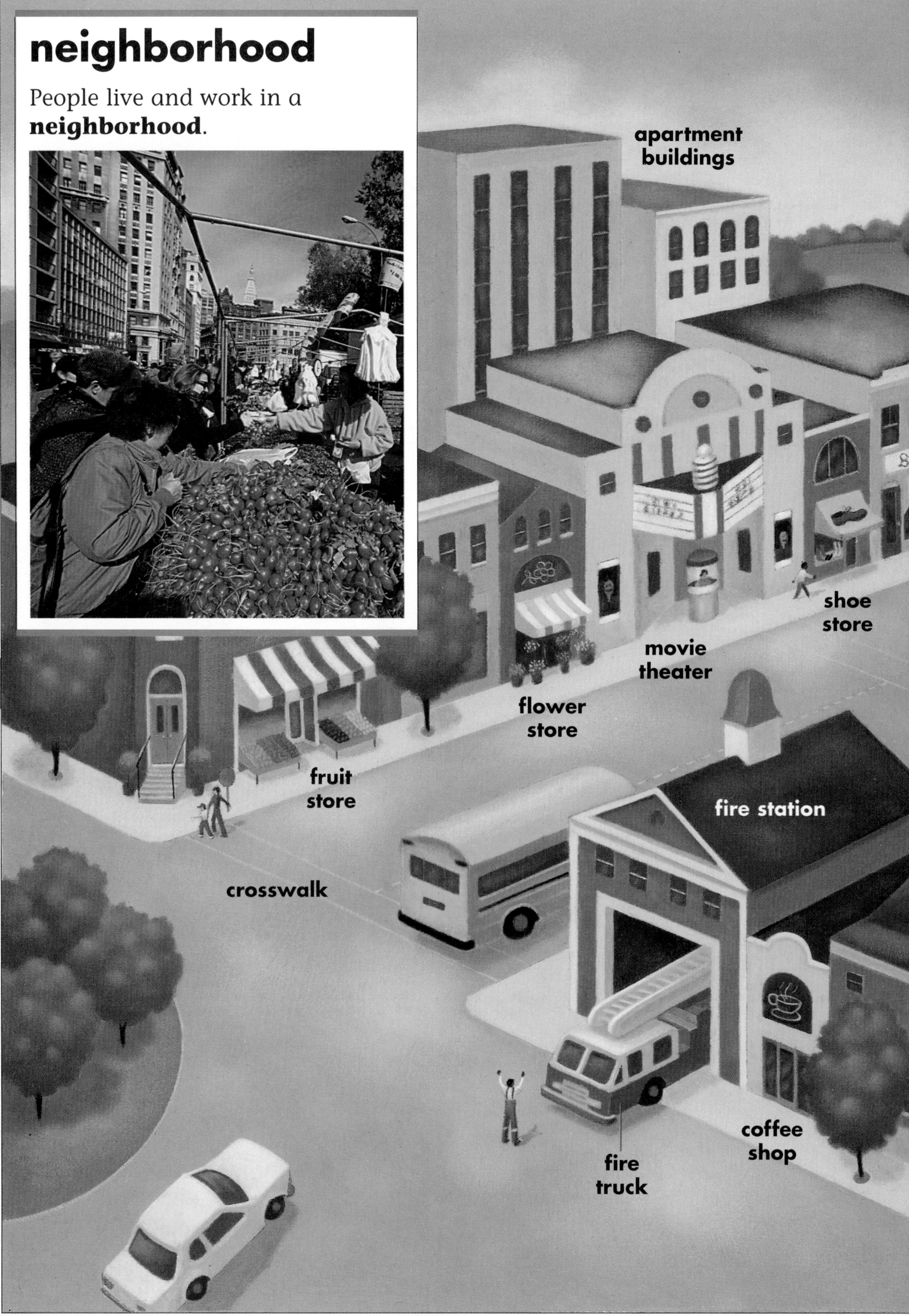

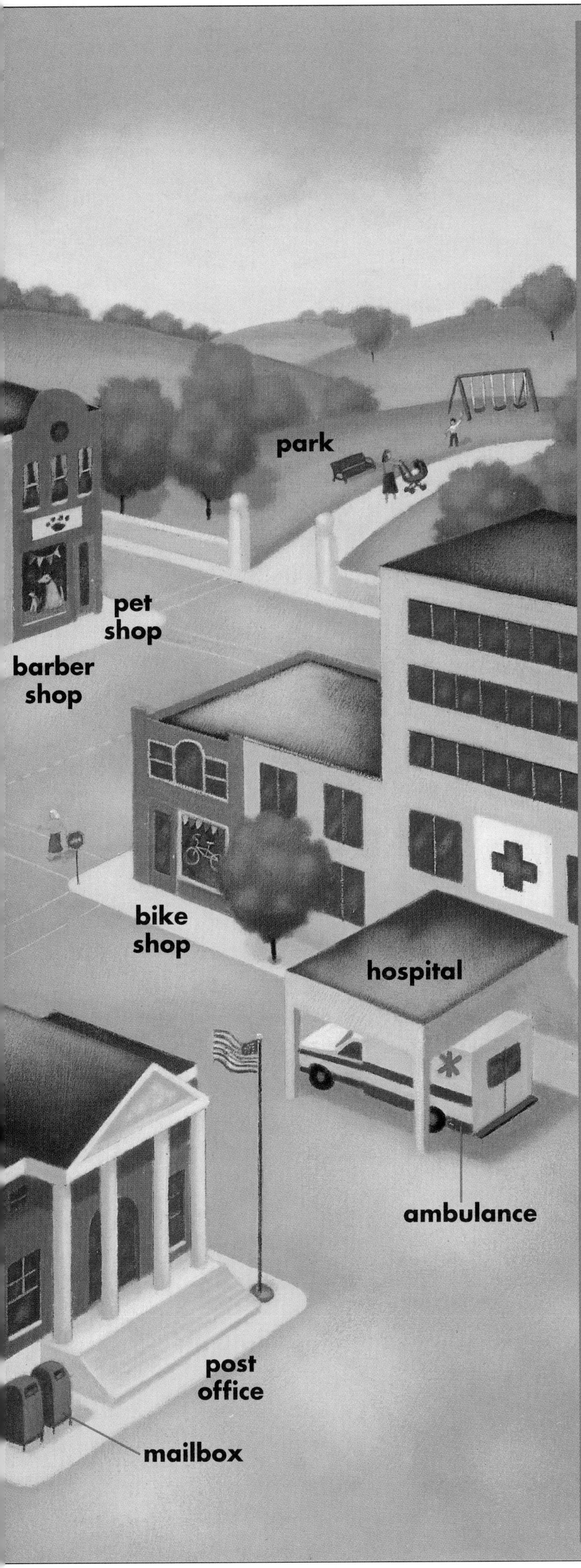

park

pet shop

barber shop

bike shop

hospital

ambulance

post office

mailbox

How do you get from the pet shop to the bike shop?

1. Walk out of the pet shop.

2. Walk past the barber shop.

3. Go by the shoe store.

4. Stop in front of the movie theater.

5. Cross the street at the crosswalk.

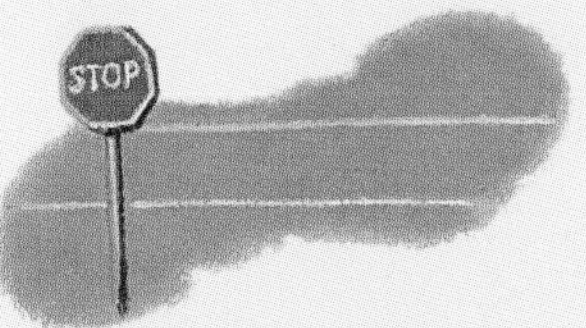

6. Go into the bike shop.

A B C D E F G H I J K L M **N** O P Q R S T U V W X Y Z

newspaper

A **newspaper** is full of information.

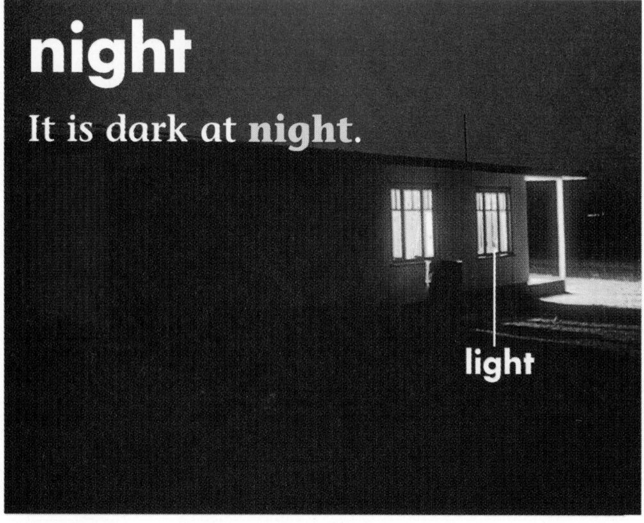

night

It is dark at **night**.

not

I am **not** hot.
I am cold.

nothing

There is **nothing** in this dish.

now

It is raining **now**!

number

A **number** shows how many things there are.

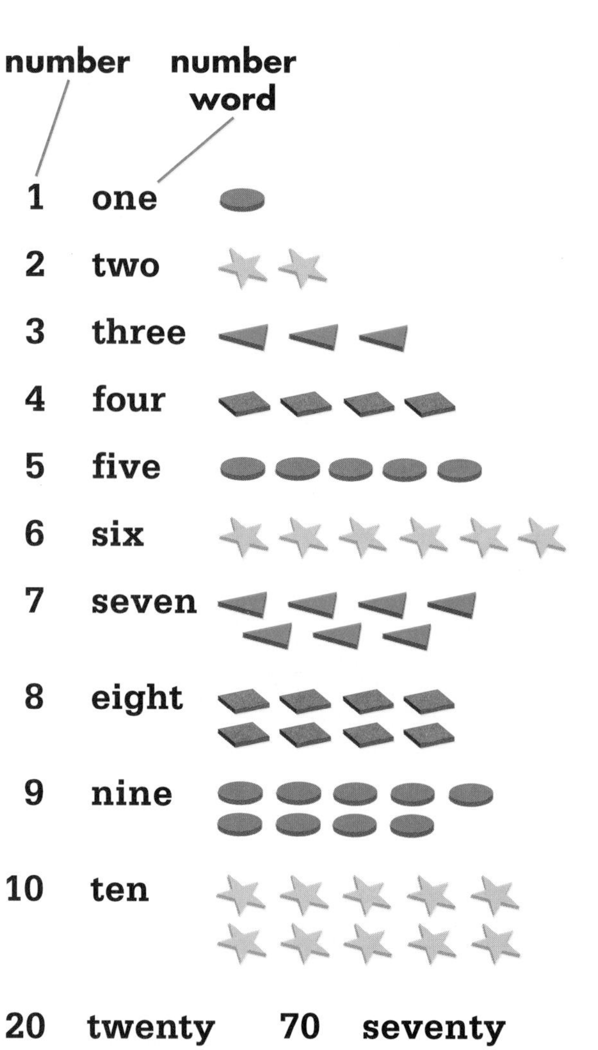

20	twenty	70	seventy
30	thirty	80	eighty
40	forty	90	ninety
50	fifty	100	one hundred
60	sixty	1000	one thousand

Oo

often

I **often** eat fruit for a snack.

observe

You can **observe** flowers in the country.

oil

We use **oil** to make popcorn.

ocean

Oceans cover much of the Earth. The water in oceans is salty.

open

1. Let me **open** the door for you.

2. We like to drive with the windows **open**.

office

The secretary works in the school **office**.

a b c d e f g h i j k l m n o p q r s t u v w x y z

A B C D E F G H I J K L M N O P Q R S T U V W X Y Z

opposite

Things that are the **opposite** of each other are very different.

above **below**

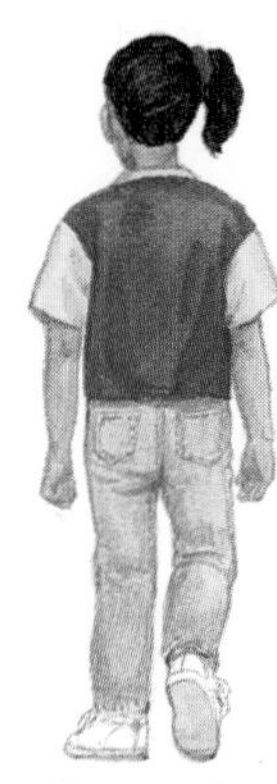

front **back**

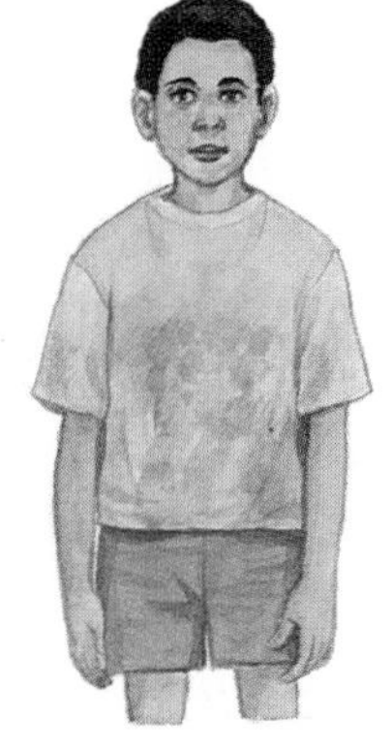

clean **dirty**

hard **soft**

empty **full**

light **heavy**

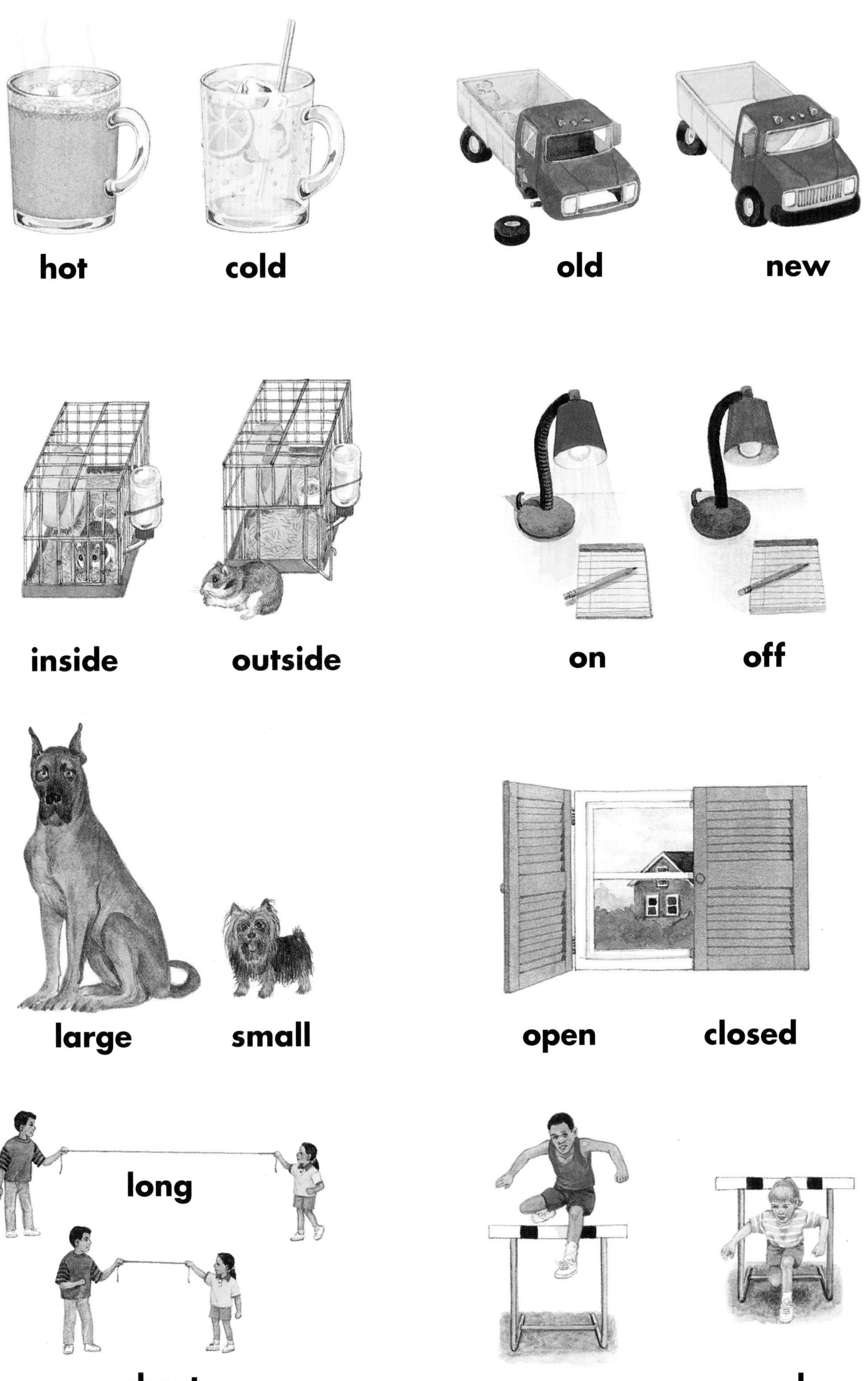
hot
cold
old
new
inside
outside
on
off
large
small
open
closed
long
short
over
under

orchestra

The musicians in the **orchestra** play their instruments together.

order

You can put things in **order**.

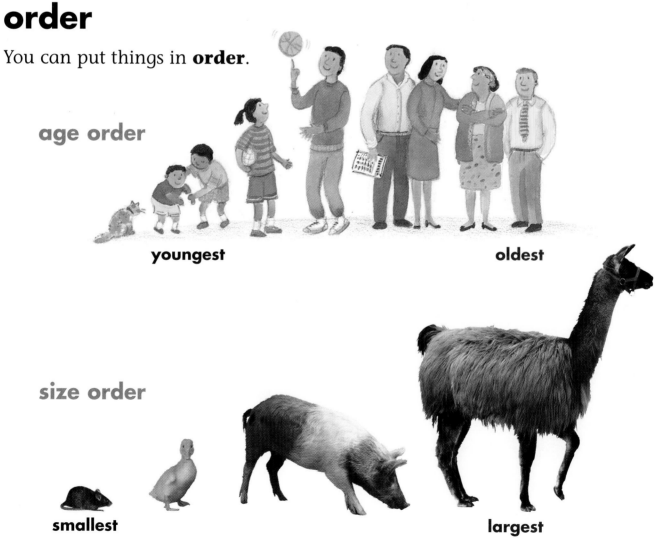

age order

youngest

oldest

size order

smallest

largest

Pp

pack

1. A **pack** is a group of wolves or dogs.

2. I **pack** my suitcase to go on a trip.

page

I like the picture on this **page**.

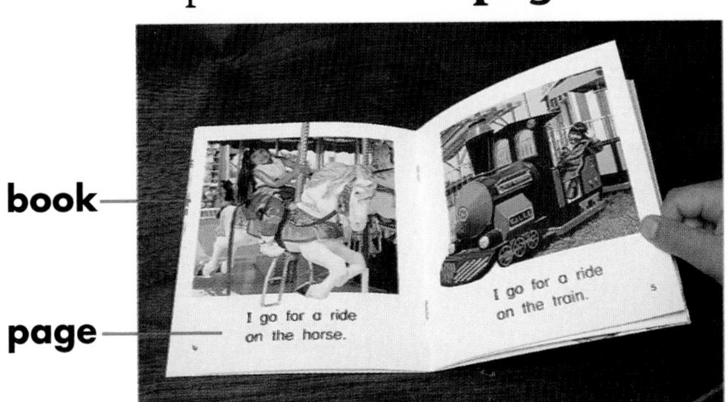

pail

You can pour sand into a **pail**.

pain

Ouch! I have a **pain** in my tooth.

paint

1. This can is full of red **paint**.

2. The painter will **paint** this chair red.

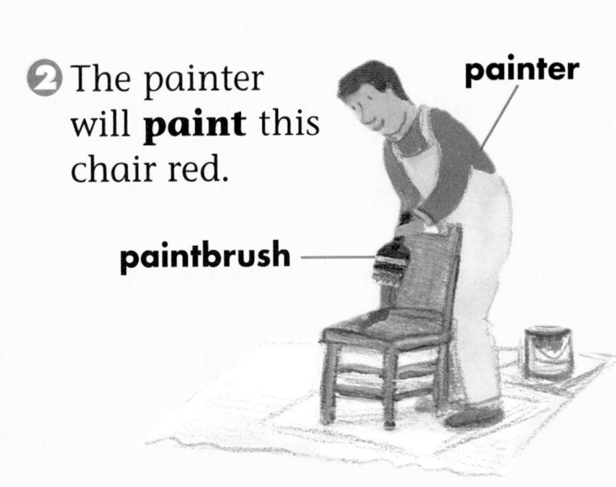

A B C D E F G H I J K L M N O P Q R S T U V W X Y Z

pair

This is a new **pair** of boots.

paper

You can write on **paper**.

Dear Nana,
Thank you for the gift. See you soon.

Love,
Jill

parade

We love the Chinese New Year **parade**!

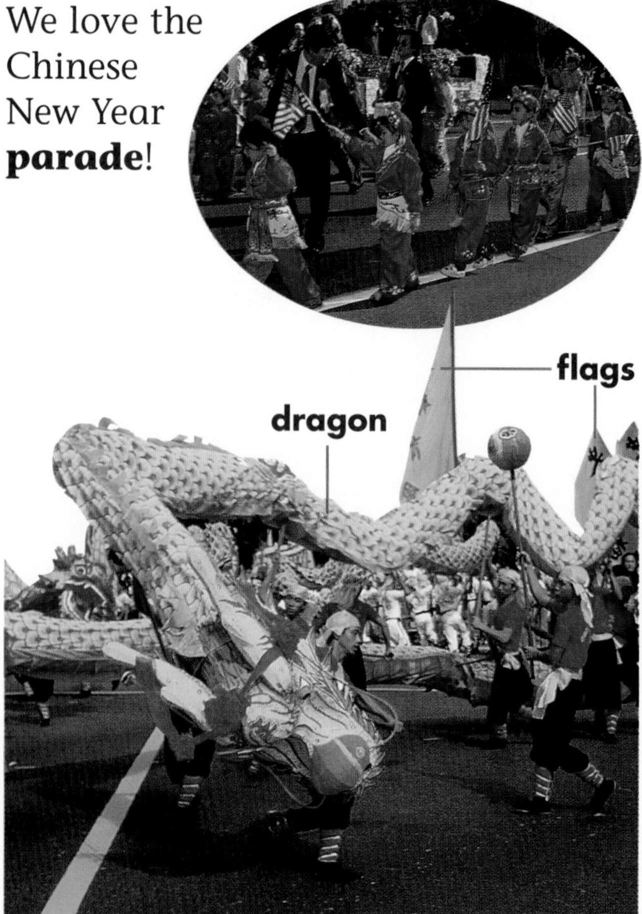

paragraph

A **paragraph** is a group of sentences. They tell about the same main idea.

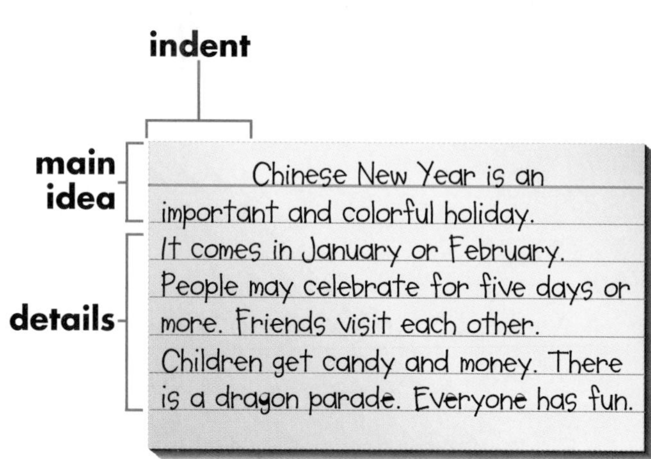

indent
main idea
details
Chinese New Year is an important and colorful holiday. It comes in January or February. People may celebrate for five days or more. Friends visit each other. Children get candy and money. There is a dragon parade. Everyone has fun.

parent

A **parent** is the mother or father of a child.

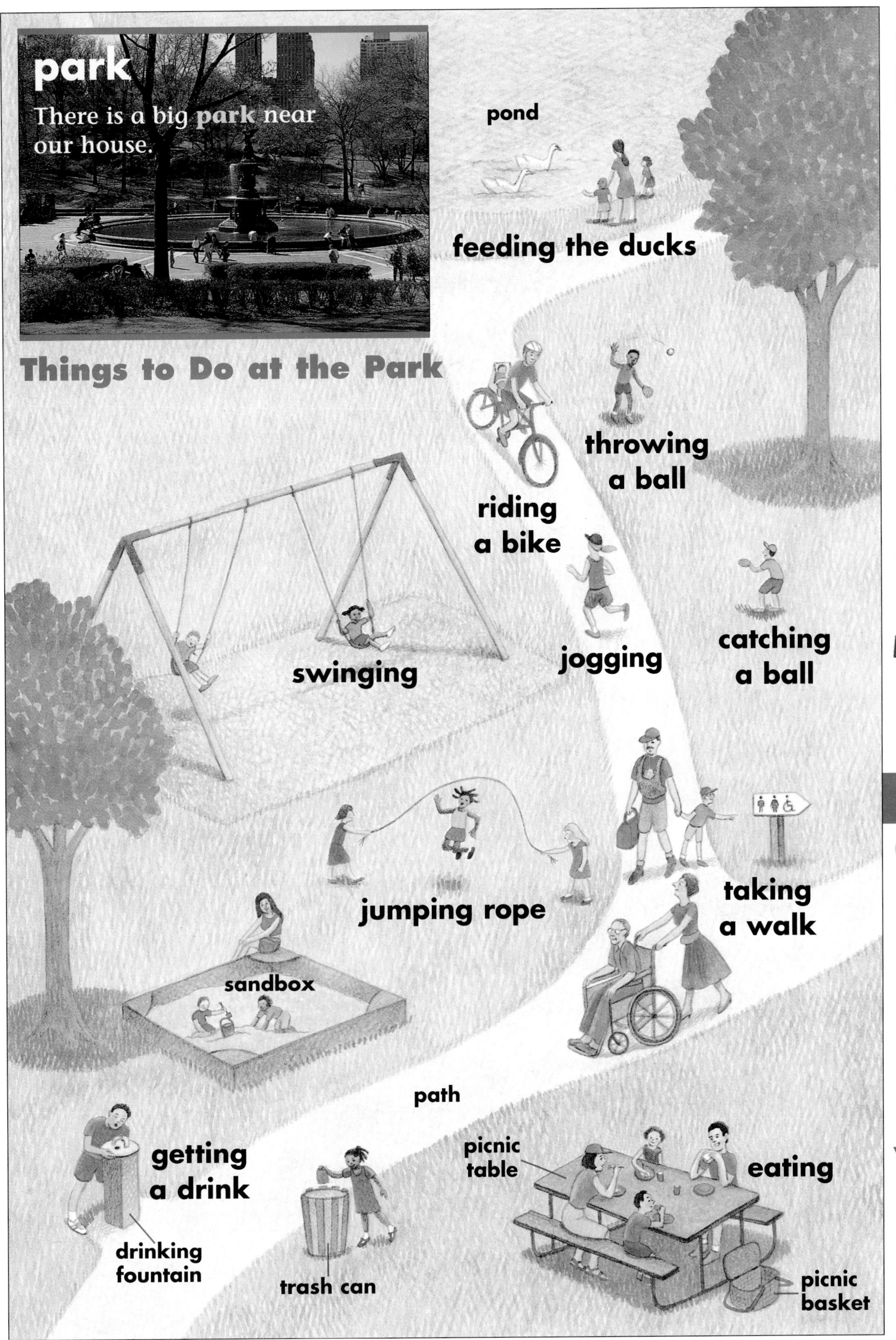

a b c d e f g h i j k l m n o p q r s t u v w x y z

A B C D E F G H I J K L M N O P Q R S T U V W X Y Z

part

One **part** of this circle is blue.

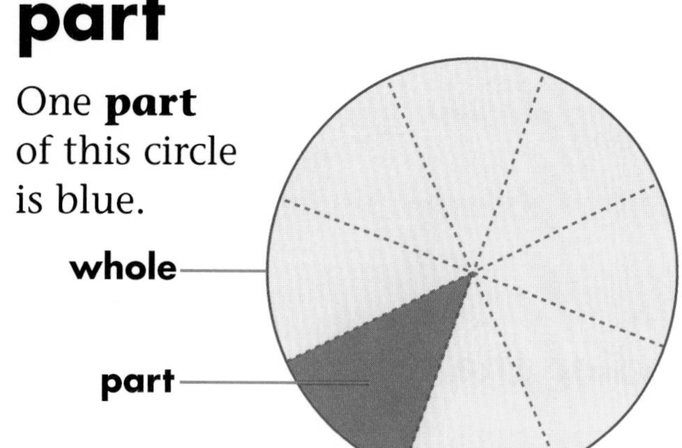

party

Our class has a **party** for Valentine's Day.

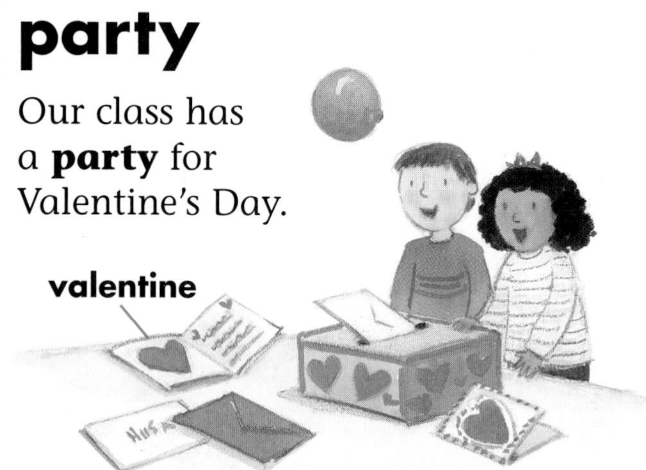

past

In the **past**, I was a baby.

path

We ride on the bike **path**.

pattern

What **pattern** do you see?

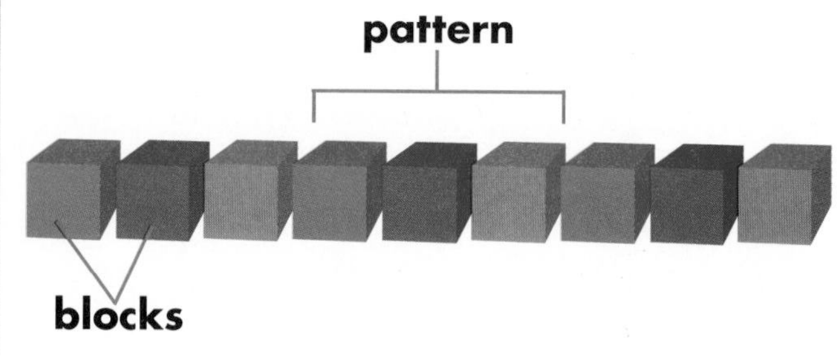

pay

You **pay** money to buy things.

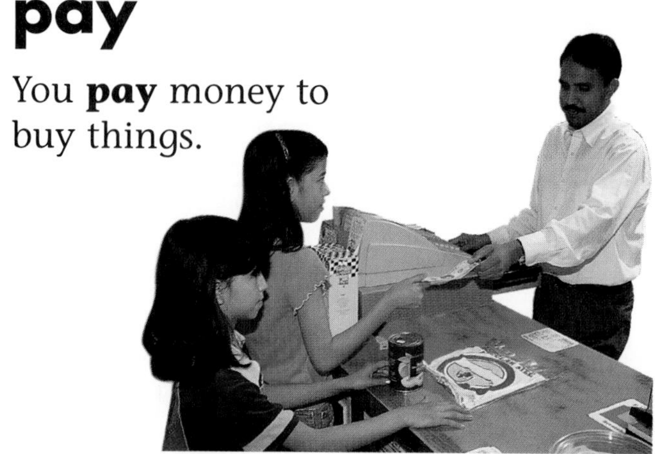

period

Put a **period** at the end of a sentence.

person

One **person** is teaching the other **people**.

person

people

pet

You must feed and take care of a **pet**.

dog

goldfish

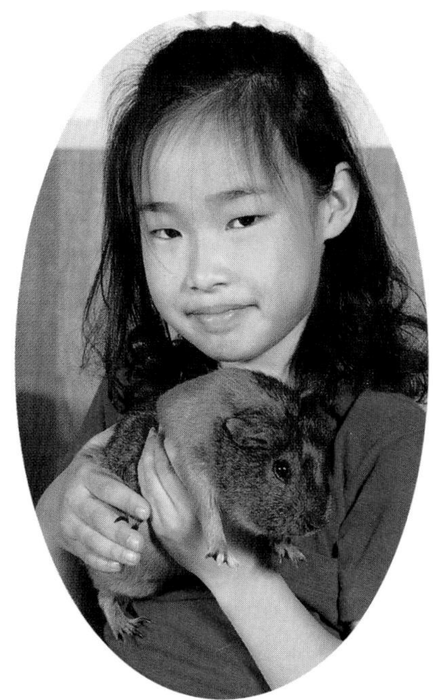

guinea pig

hamster

rabbit

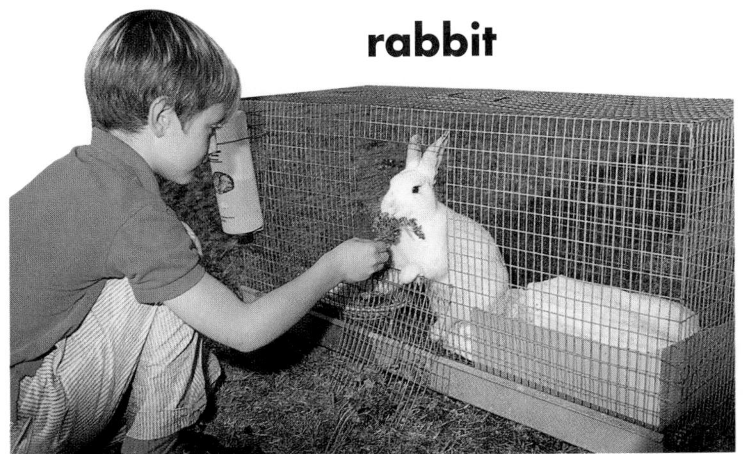

bird

A B C D E F G H I J K L M N O P Q R S T U V W X Y Z

phone

The boys talk on the **phone**.

piano

You can play music on a **piano**.

picture

This is a **picture** of some farmers.

piece

Would you like a **piece** of bread?

pile

This is a big **pile** of leaves.

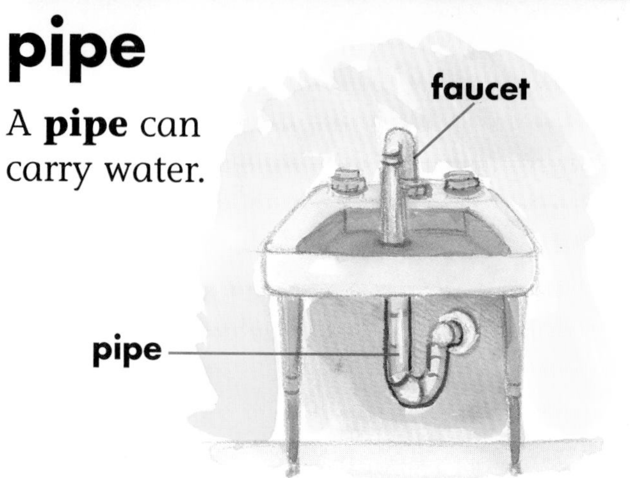

pipe

A **pipe** can carry water.

plain

She will choose the **plain** socks.

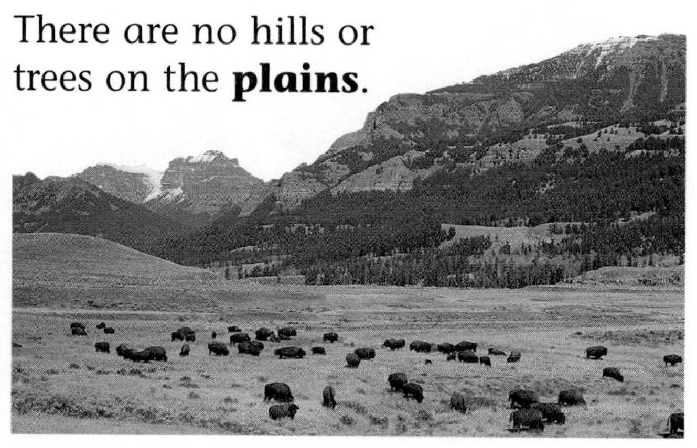

plains

There are no hills or trees on the **plains**.

plant

Some **plants** grow in the ground.
Some plants grow in water.

leaves
berries
branch
trunk
tree
bush
leaf
stem
vine
fronds
fern
blade
grass
air bladder
seaweed

poem

This **poem** has rhyming words.

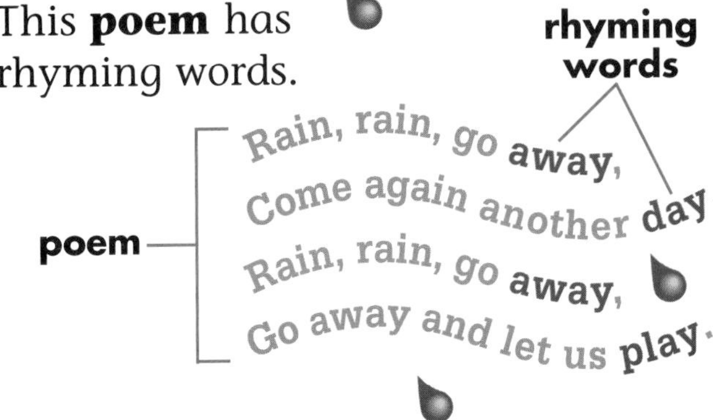

rhyming words
poem
Rain, rain, go away,
Come again another day.
Rain, rain, go away,
Go away and let us play.

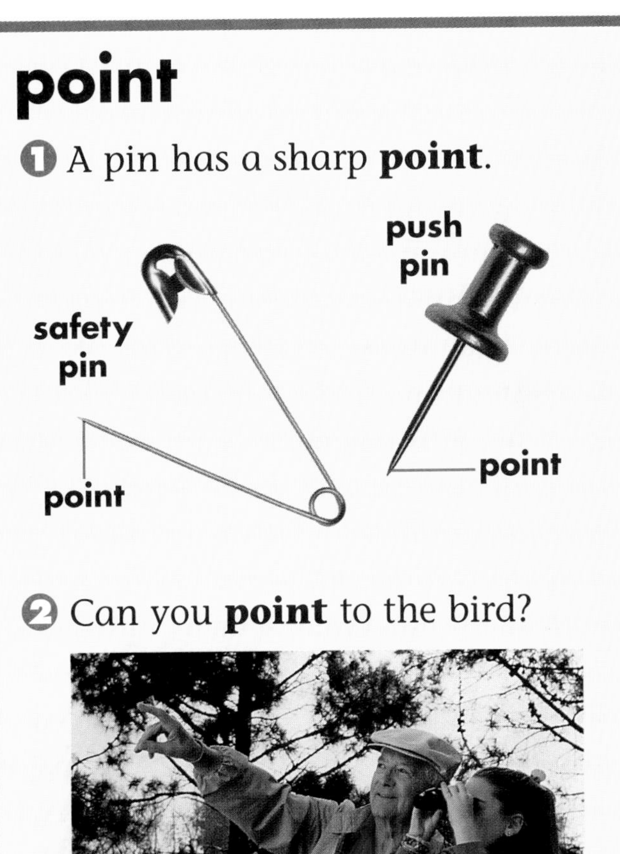

point

❶ A pin has a sharp **point**.

❷ Can you **point** to the bird?

pollution

Pollution hurts the air, land, water, and living things.

a b c d e f g h i j k l m n o p q r s t u v w x y z

practice

The boy will **practice** over and over.

product

Wood is a **product** from a tree.

protect

A helmet can **protect** your head.

pull

He will **pull** the wagon to the grocery store.

puppet

These **puppets** act out a play.

push

You can **push** something, or you can pull it.

put

She **put** the book in her locker.

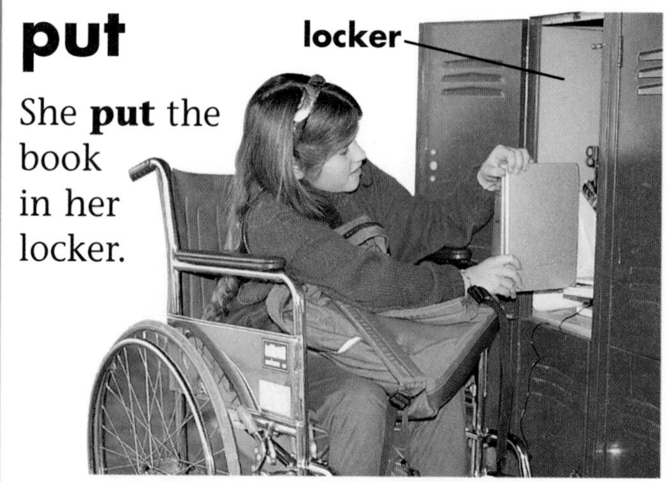

puzzle

Mei is putting the **puzzle** together.

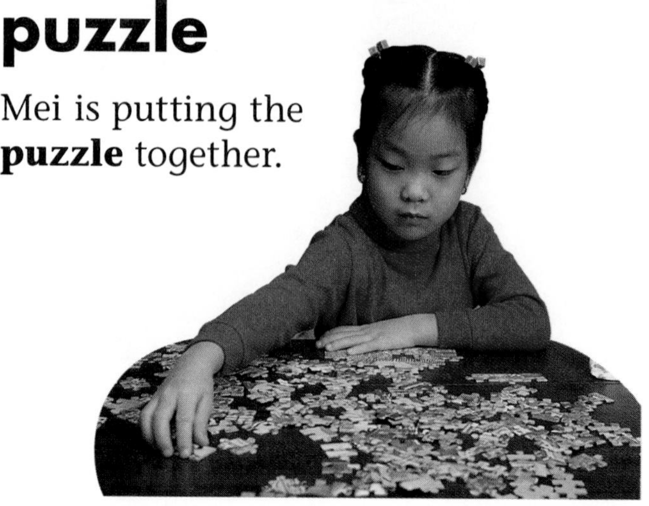

Qq

quickly

Come to the phone **quickly**. It's your mom calling.

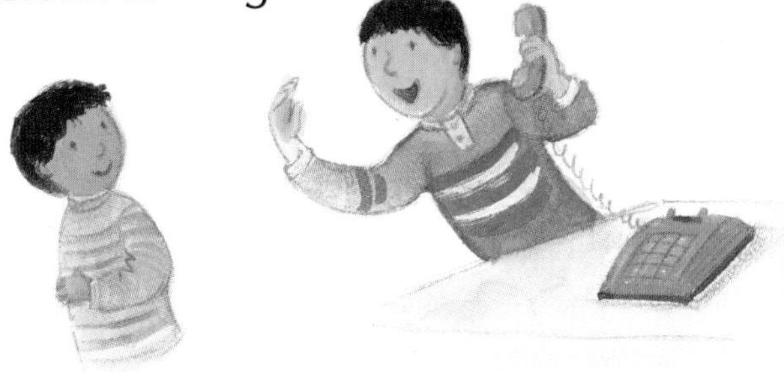

question

You ask a **question**. You get an answer.

What's your name?
question
My name is Lisa.

I'm 7. How old are you?
question mark
I'm 7, too!

Do you like to play ball?
exclamation mark
Yes, I do. Let's play!

quiet

Shh. This is a **quiet** place.

quilt

The **quilt** will keep her warm.

quite

It is **quite** cold today!

A B C D E F G H I J K L M N O P Q R S T U V W X Y Z

Rr

rain

You use an umbrella in the **rain**.

race

Manuel will win this **race**.

rainbow

There is a **rainbow** after the storm.

radio

You can listen to music on a **radio**.

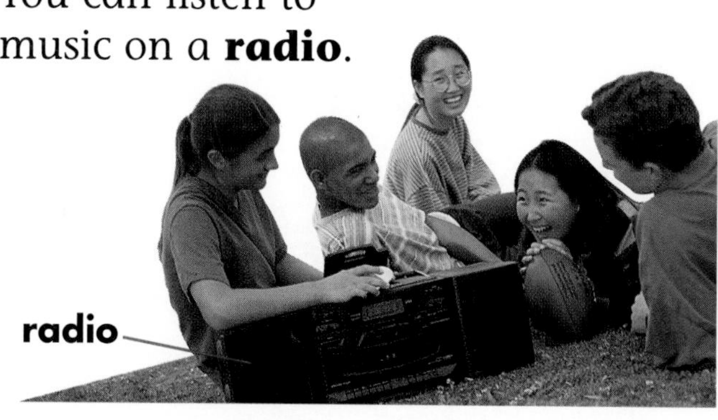

railroad

Trains carry people and cargo along a **railroad**.

rain forest

A tropical **rain forest** is a hot, wet place. Many plants grow there.

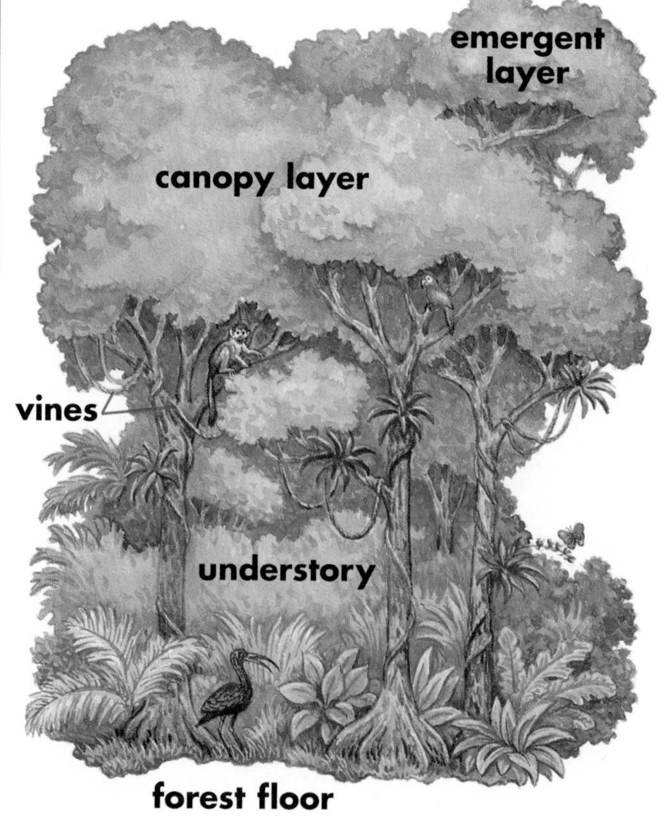

raise

They all **raise** their hands to answer the question.

rectangle

A **rectangle** has four corners, two long sides, and two short sides.

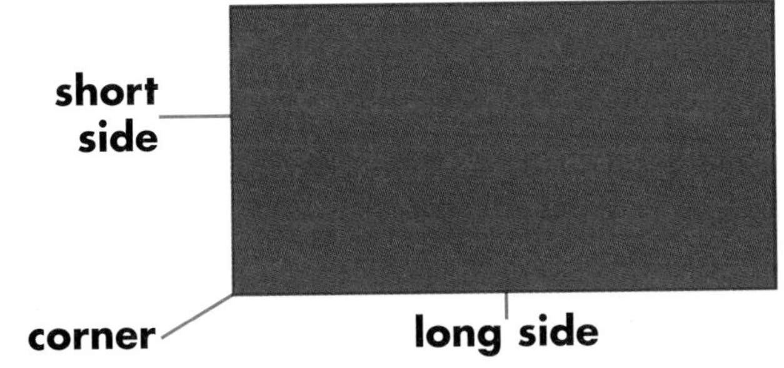

recycle

It is good to **recycle** paper and cans. They can be used again.

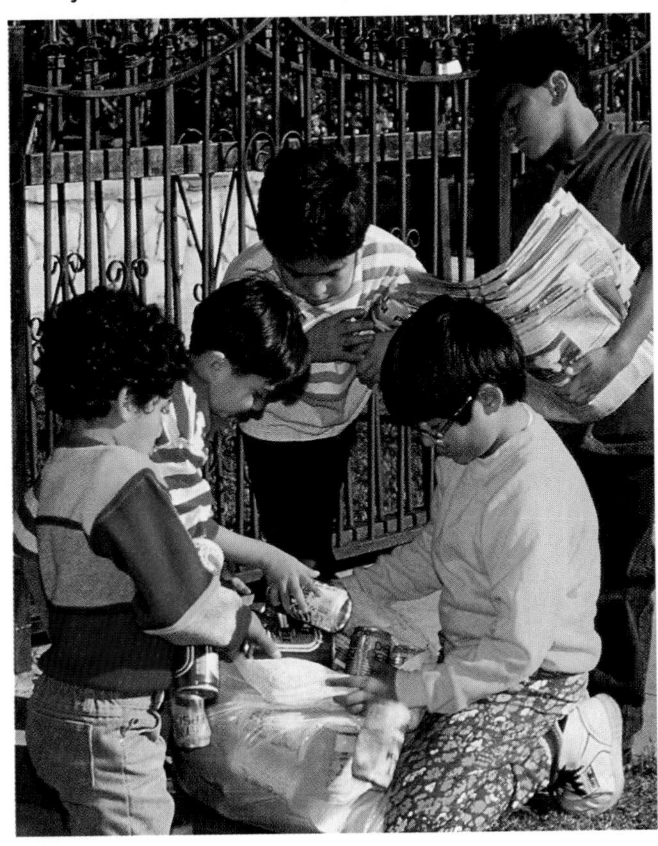

remember

Remember to do your homework tonight.

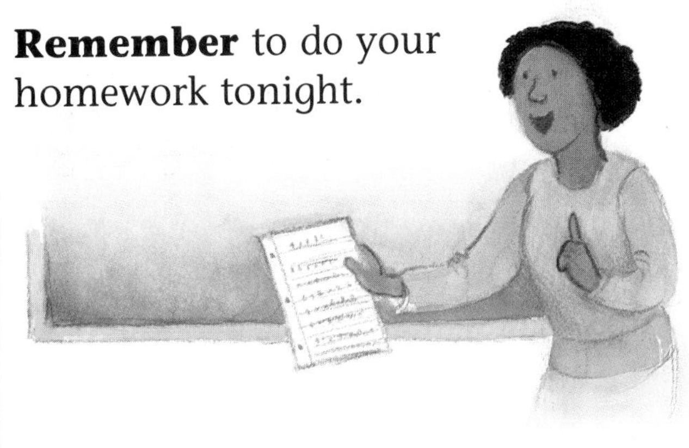

reptile

Most **reptiles** have dry, scaly skin.

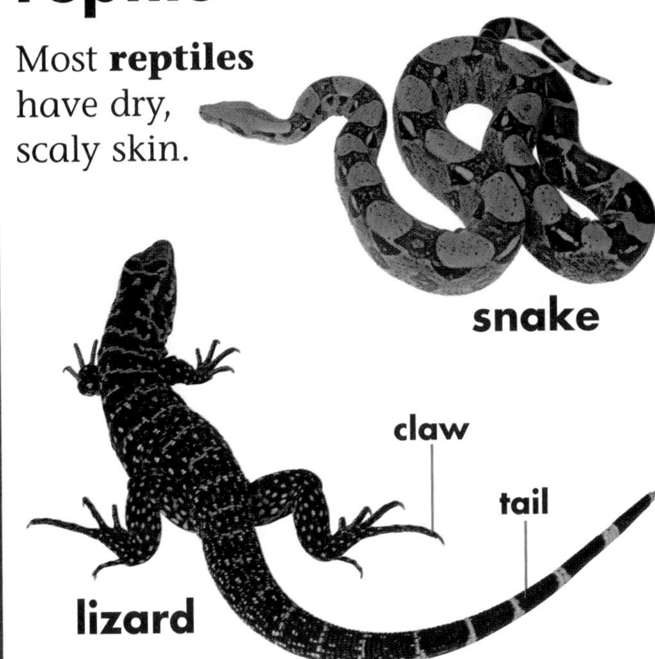

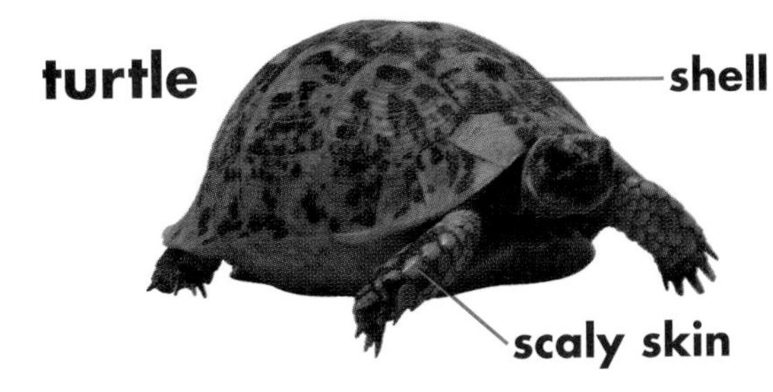

restaurant

Eating in a **restaurant** is fun.

In the Kitchen

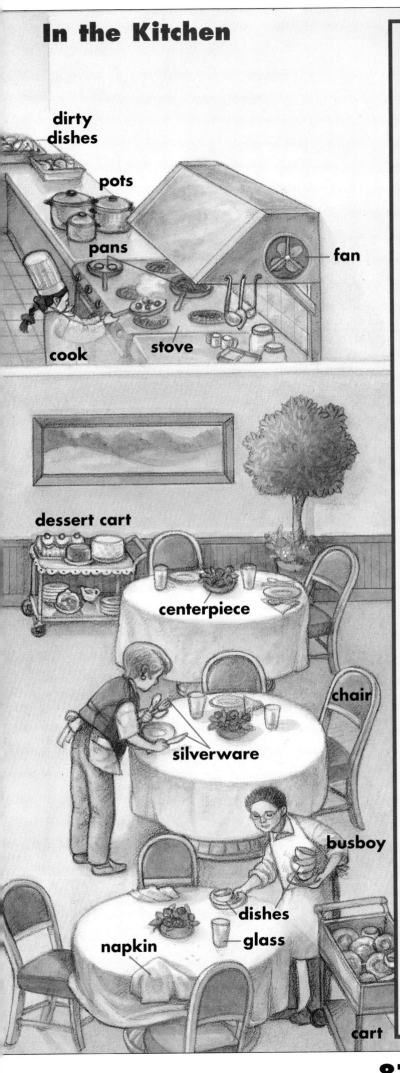

dirty dishes
pots
pans
fan
cook
stove
dessert cart
centerpiece
chair
silverware
busboy
dishes
glass
napkin
cart

What did they do at the restaurant?

He paid the bill for dinner.

They ate dinner in the kitchen.

He washed all the dishes.

She went home to her family.

A B C D E F G H I J K L M N O P Q R S T U V W X Y Z

return

We need to **return** this shirt. It is too big for him.

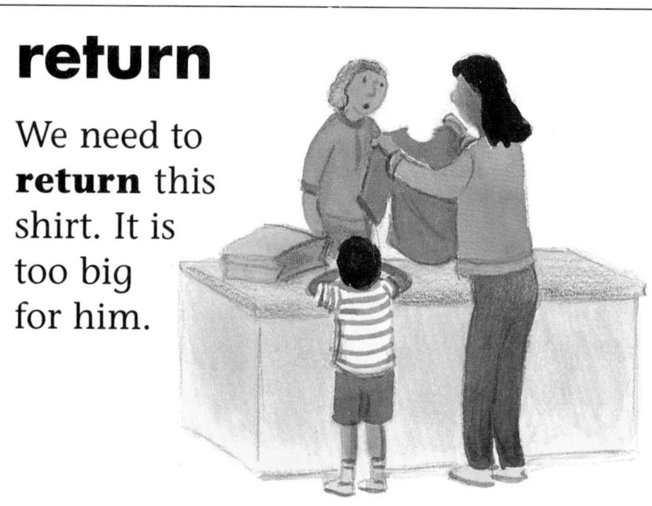

river

This **river** is in Egypt. It is the Nile.

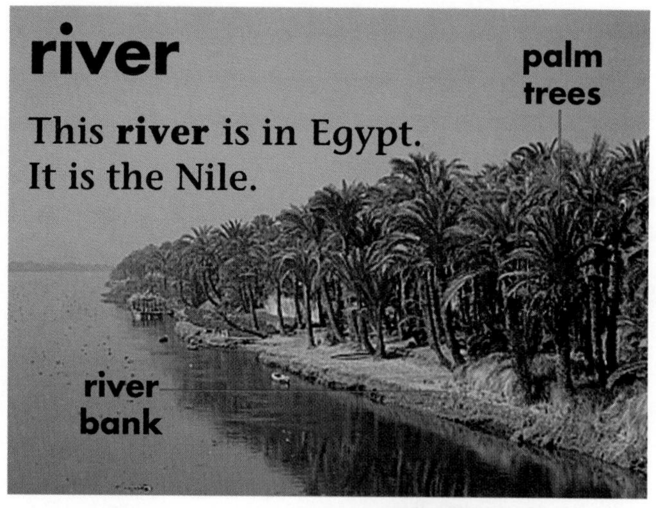

ride

They like to **ride** their bikes.

rock

A **rock** is always hard. It comes from the earth.

right

1. Turn **right** at the next street.

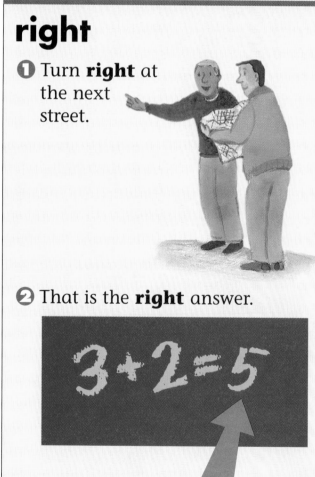

2. That is the **right** answer.

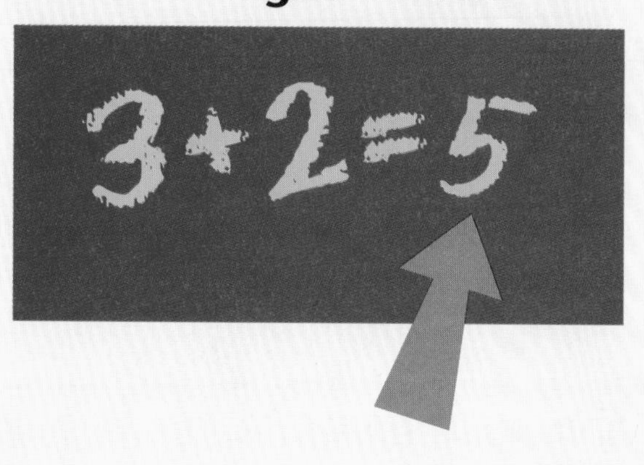

roll

1. This **roll** tastes so good!

2. He can **roll** the ball down the lane.

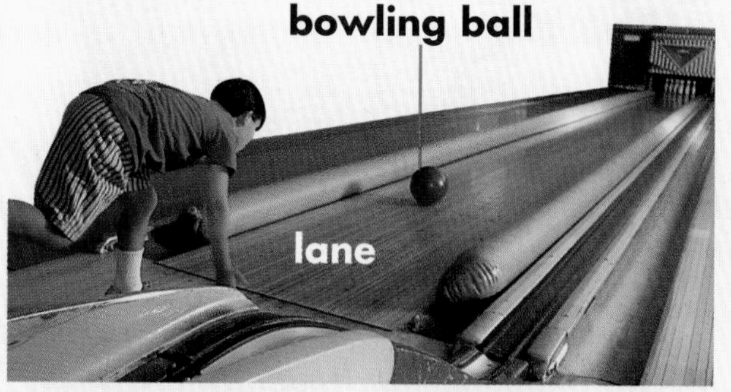

root

The **root** of a plant grows under the ground.

rough

The bark of a tree feels **rough** when you touch it.

row

1. The front **row** is close to the teacher.

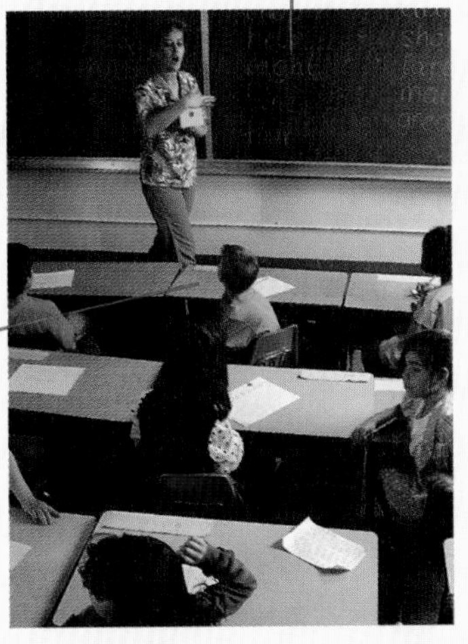

2. You use oars to **row** a boat across the lake.

rule

Always raise your hand before you speak. That's the **rule** at school.

ruler

You can use a **ruler** to measure something.

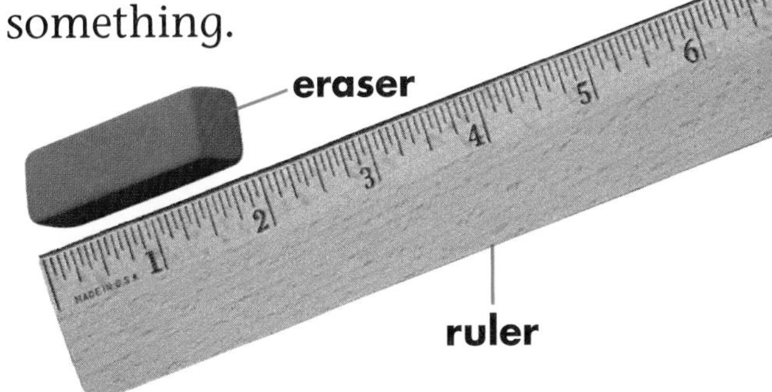

run

It's fun to **run** on the beach.

rush

Don't **rush**. Take your time to do your work.

a b c d e f g h i j k l m n o p q **r** s t u v w x y z

Ss

sack

Can you lift a **sack** of potatoes?

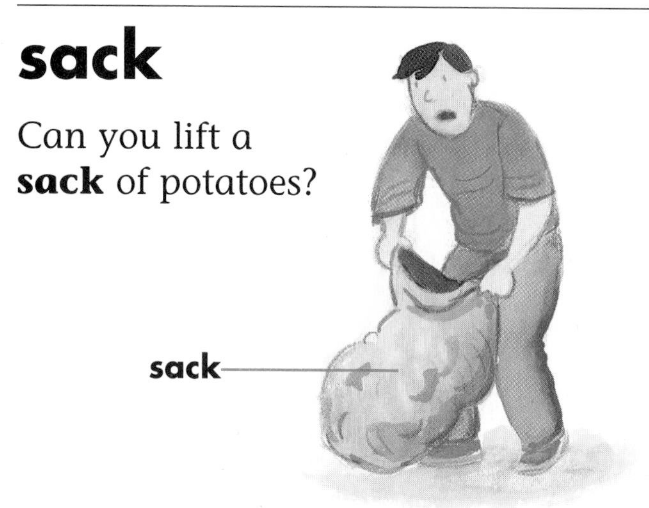

safe

Wear your helmet to be **safe**!

sailboat

You can sail a **sailboat** on a lake.

sail

sailboat

sale

This house is for **sale**. Who will buy it?

salt

Salt can add flavor to food.

same

Alexa and I have the **same** kind of cap.

save

You can **save** money in a bank.

say

What did you **say**? I can't hear you.

scale

You can weigh food on a **scale**.

scare

A mouse can **scare** an elephant!

scene

This painting shows a country **scene**.

school

It's time for **school**!

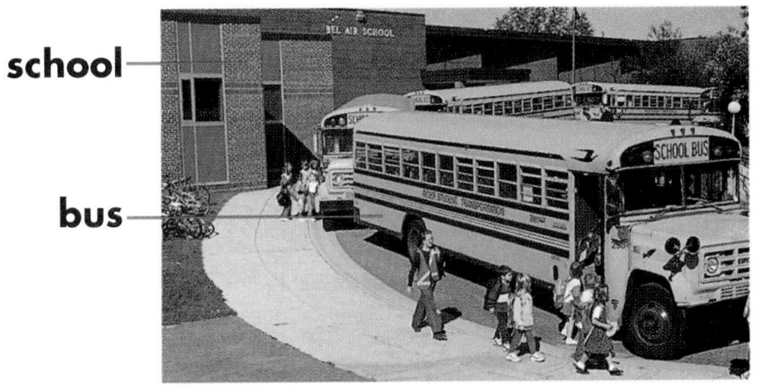

classroom

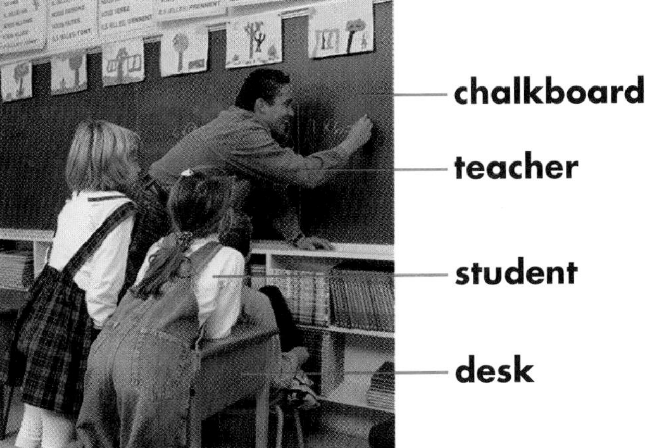

library

playground

a b c d e f g h i j k l m n o p q r s t u v w x y z

sea

The **sea** covers much of the Earth. The water in the sea is salty.

Animals and Plants

A B C D E F G H I J K L M N O P Q R S T U V W X Y Z

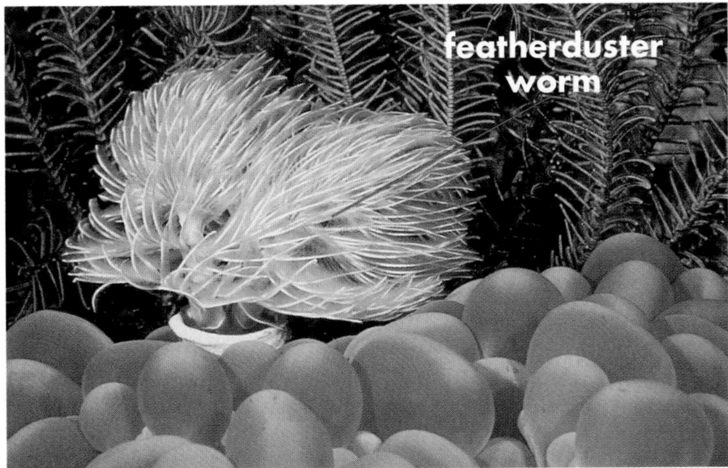

How do animals breathe in the sea?

Fish can breathe underwater through their gills.

Whales must come up to the top. They breathe through a blowhole.

Seals must come up to the top, too. They use their lungs to breathe.

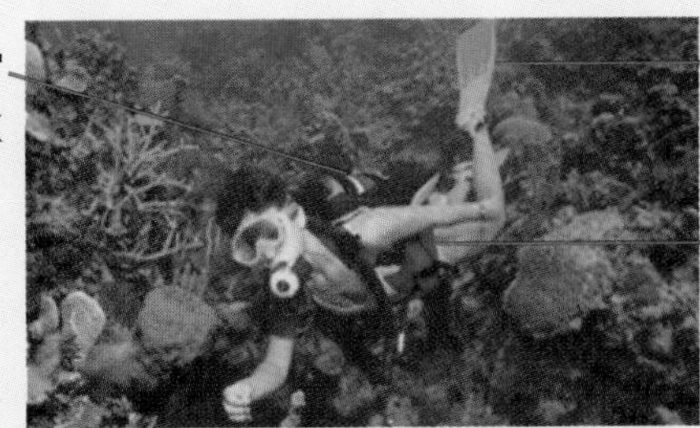

A diver can breathe through a tube. The tube is connected to a tank of air.

seashore

Many plants and animals live along the **seashore**.

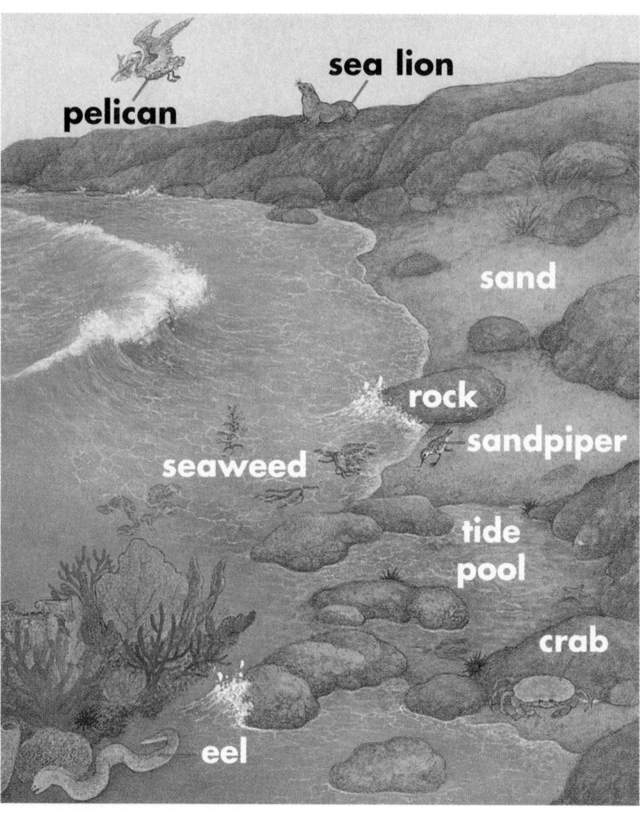

seasons

The four **seasons** are spring, summer, fall, and winter.

secret

You can tell a friend a **secret**.

see

He needs glasses to **see** well.

seed

A plant grows from a **seed** in the ground.

sell

They **sell** drinks at a stand.

send

You can **send** a postcard to say hello.

senses

Our **senses** help us see, hear, taste, smell, and touch.

sentence

A **sentence** starts with a capital letter. Some sentences end with a period.

capital letter

period

We like school.

sentence

several

Several children will do the experiment.

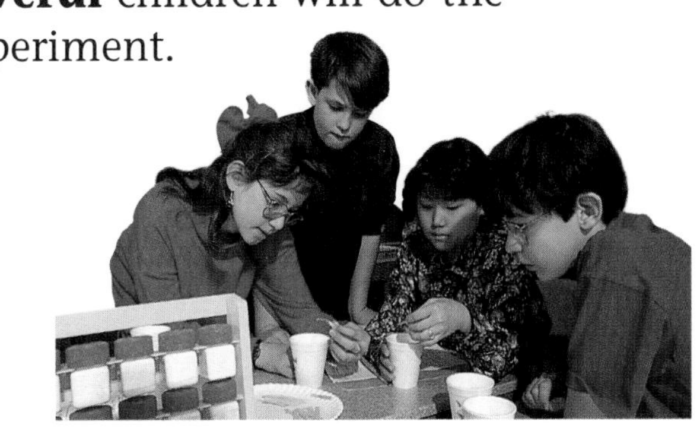

sew

You **sew** with a needle and thread.

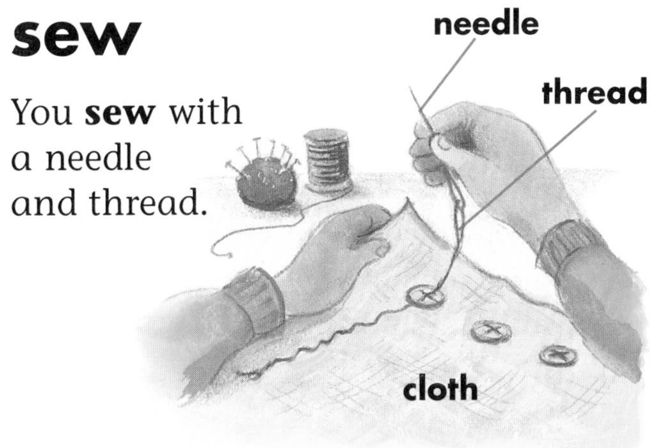

shadow

Eli can see his own **shadow**.

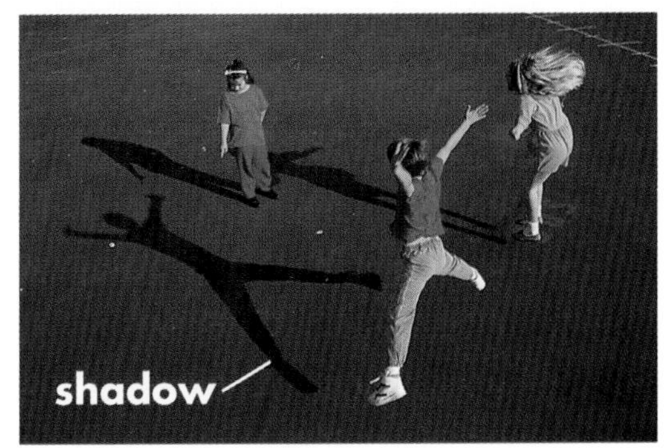

A B C D E F G H I J K L M N O P Q R S T U V W X Y Z

shape

The **shape** of a circle is round.

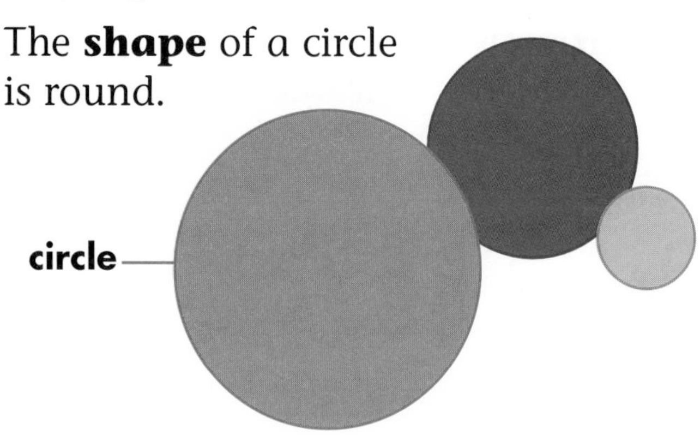

shine

The headlights **shine** on the road.

shiny

These dimes are very **shiny**.

ship

A ship travels across the sea.

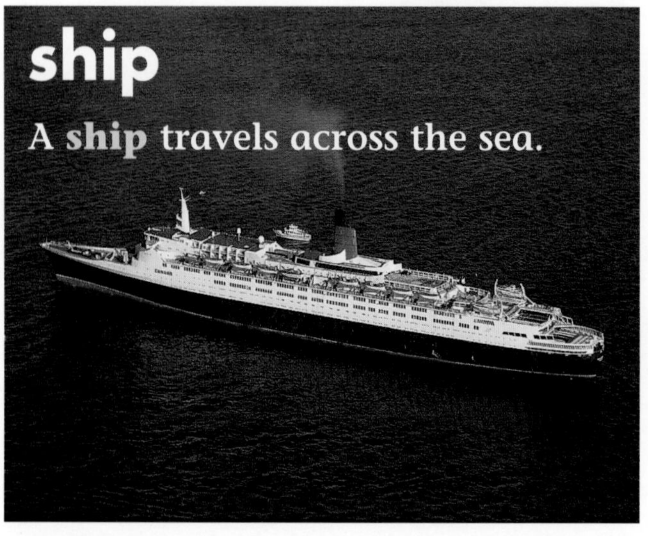

shop

1. You can **shop** for food at the grocery store.

2. You can buy a bird at the pet **shop**.

shout

We **shout** when our team wins.

show

He will **show** his new jacket to his sister.

sick

Maria is **sick** in bed.

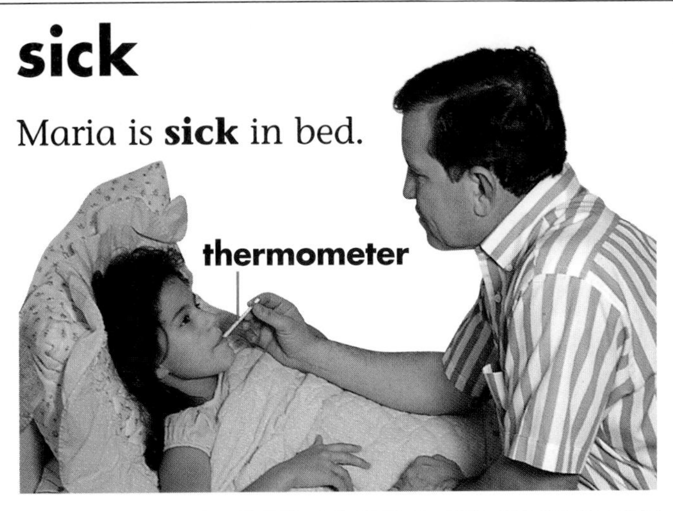

silk

This kimono is made of **silk**. It is soft and beautiful.

sign

A **sign** tells you what to do.

sing

We **sing** songs at school.

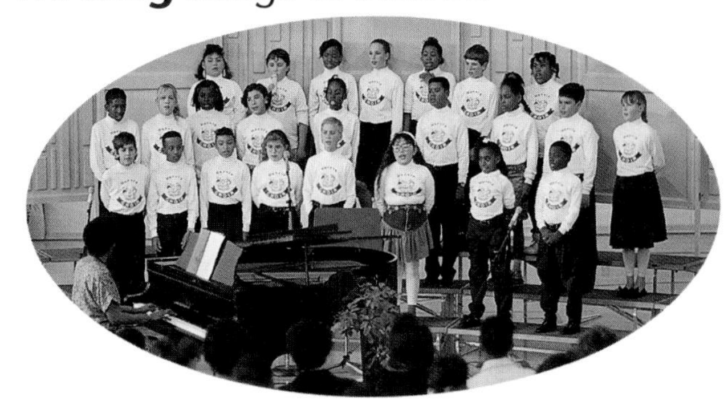

skeleton

A human **skeleton** has 206 bones.

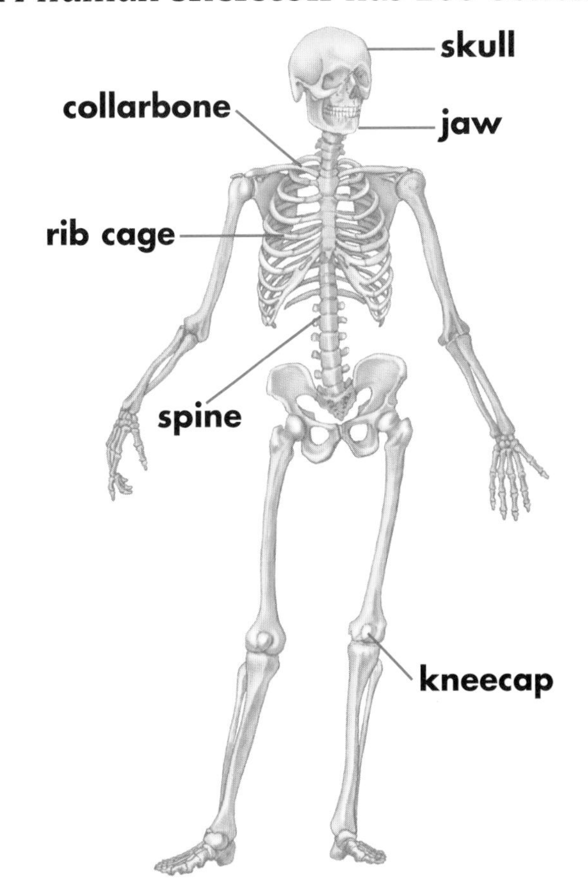

a b c d e f g h i j k l m n o p q r s t u v w x y z

sky

The **sky** is beautiful today.

slow

A snail is a very **slow** animal.

spend

You can **spend** money on ice cream.

spider

A **spider** has eight legs.

sports

It's fun to play **sports**.

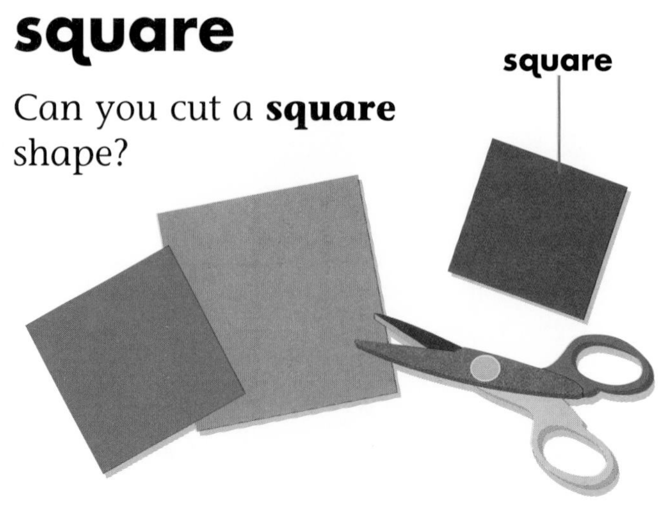

square

Can you cut a **square** shape?

star

1. A **star** in the sky is very far away.

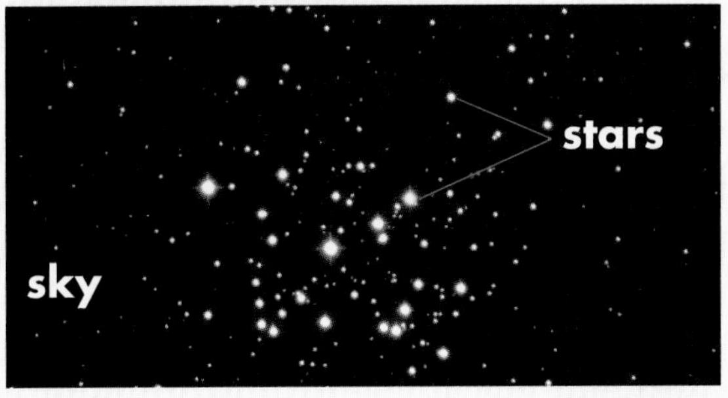

2. Carlos is the **star** of our class play.

state

California is the longest **state** in the United States.

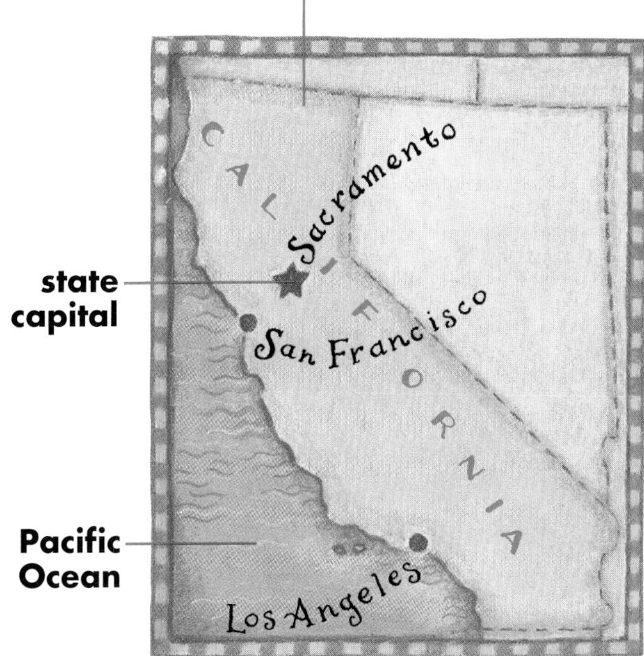

store

You can buy sneakers at the shoe **store**.

storm

It was windy and rainy during the **storm**.

story

Sara wrote a **story** about a tiger.

stretch

You **stretch** your muscles when you bend over.

a b c d e f g h i j k l m n o p q r s t u v w x y z

strong

You must be **strong** to win a game of tug-of-war.

study

We like to **study** the continents.

sun

The sun lights up the sky.

surprise

Here's a **surprise** for you!

swim

You can learn how to **swim** at a pool.

swing

1. There is a **swing** in the tree.

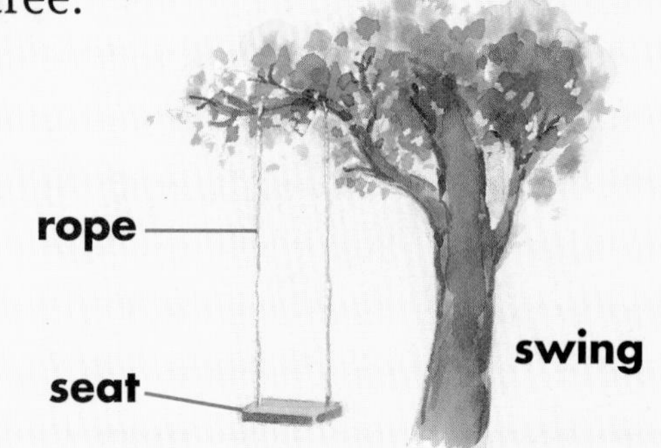

2. You can **swing** higher and higher.

syllable

Point to the first **syllable** in this word.

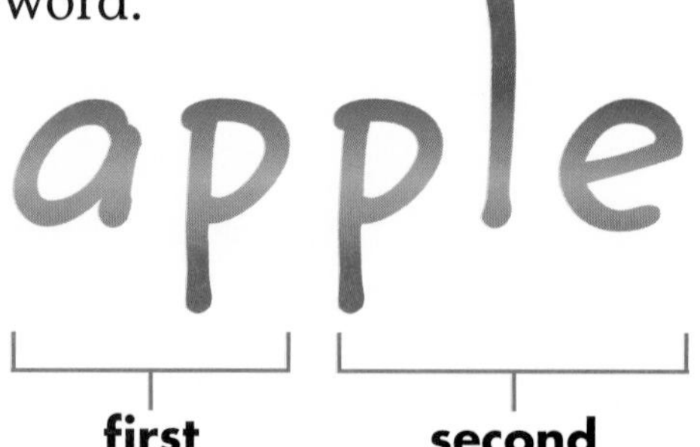

Tt

take

Please **take** this home tonight.

talk

We **talk** on the phone every Saturday.

tall

The giraffe is a **tall** animal.

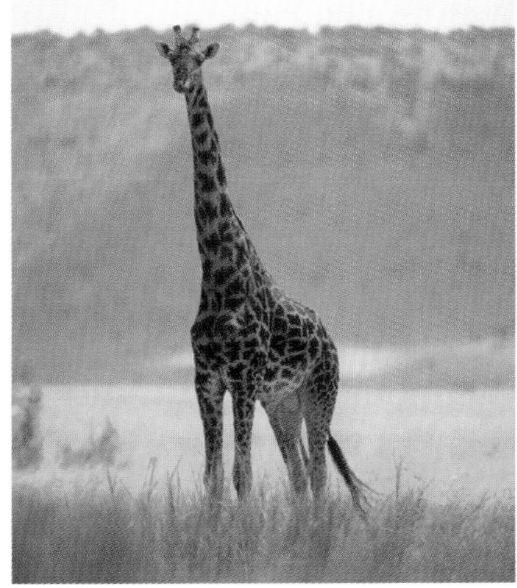

team

This is a picture of my soccer **team**.

think

How much is 5 + 5? Let me **think**.

throw

I use my arm to **throw** things.

ticket

May I have your **ticket**, please?

a b c d e f g h i j k l m n o p q r s t u v w x y z

A B C D E F G H I J K L M N O P Q R S **T** U V W X Y Z

tie

❶ You wear a **tie** around your neck.

❷ Look! I can **tie** my shoe!

time

What **time** is it? It's 4 o'clock.

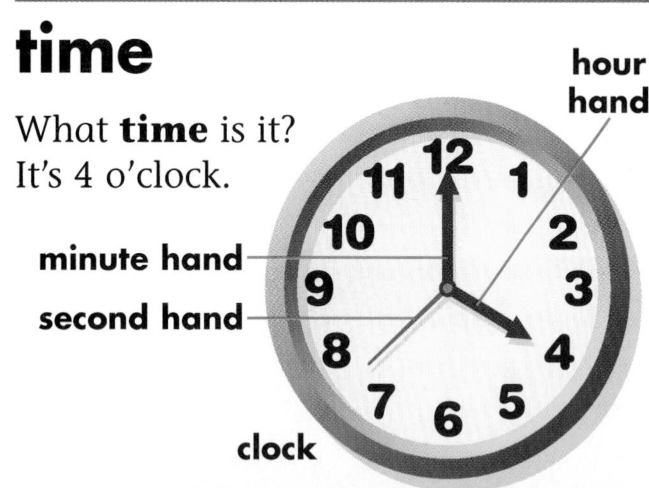

tiny

This insect is **tiny**. It is very, very small.

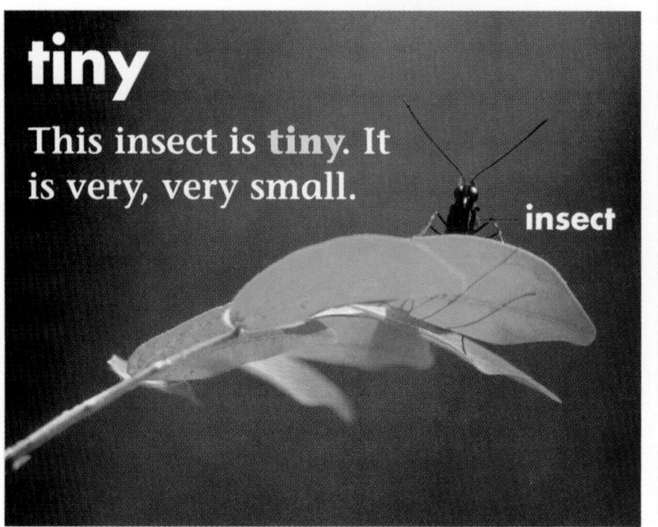

tire

This is a huge **tire**.

today

Today is Monday. I'm wearing my green pants.

tomorrow

Tomorrow will be Tuesday. I'll wear my blue skirt.

tonight

I'll take my blue skirt out of the closet **tonight**.

tool

People use **tools** to do different kinds of jobs.

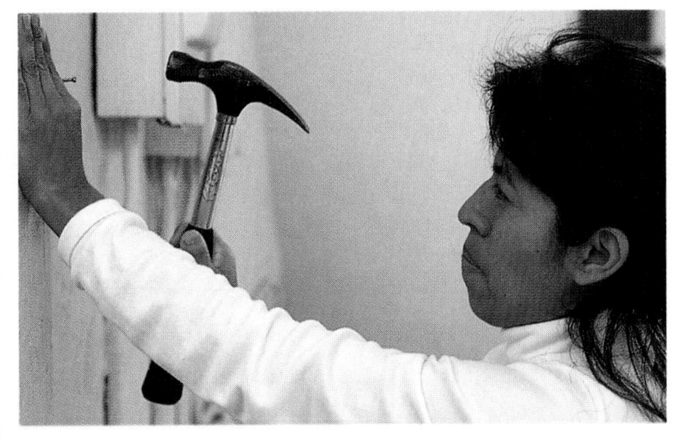

At School

At Work

In the Kitchen

In the Garden

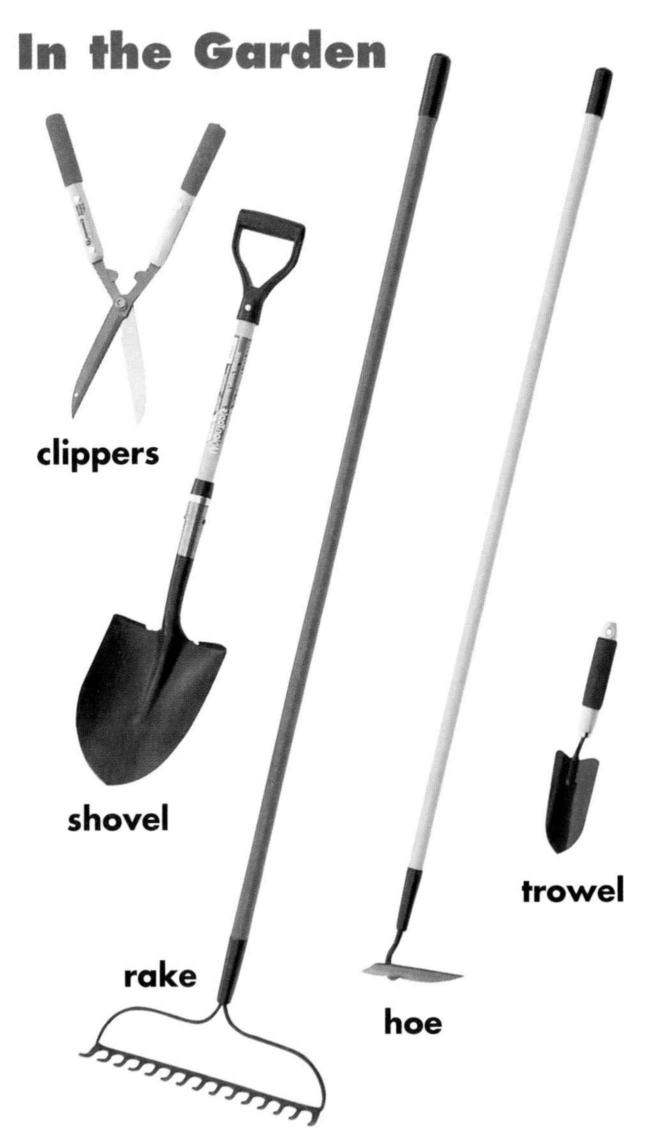

top

Write your name at the **top** of the paper.

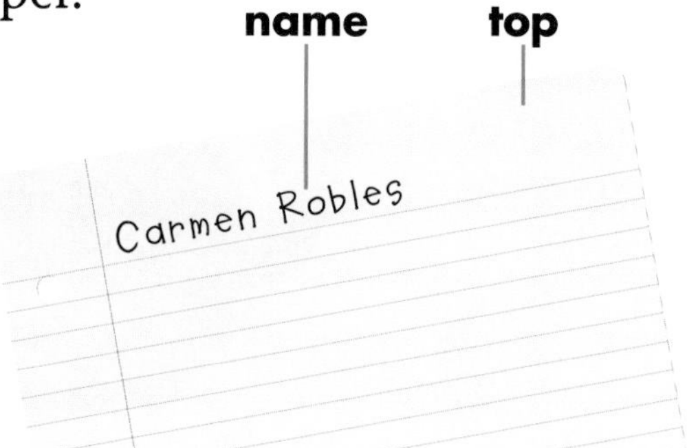

town

A **town** is smaller than a city.

track

An animal leaves a track when it walks on the ground.

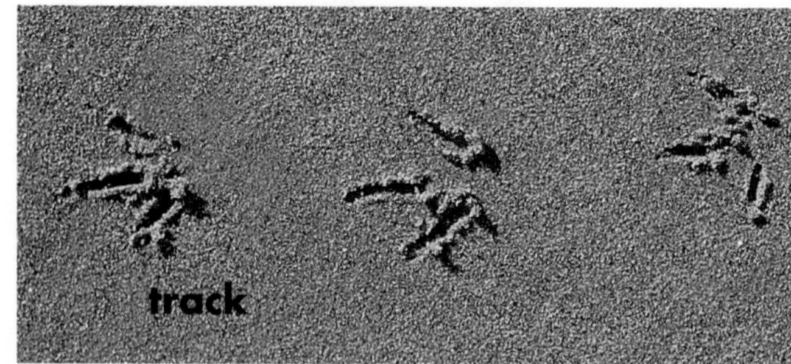

trade

Let's **trade**. You give me your toy. I will give you my toy.

tree

This **tree** has a long trunk.

triangle

A **triangle** has three sides.

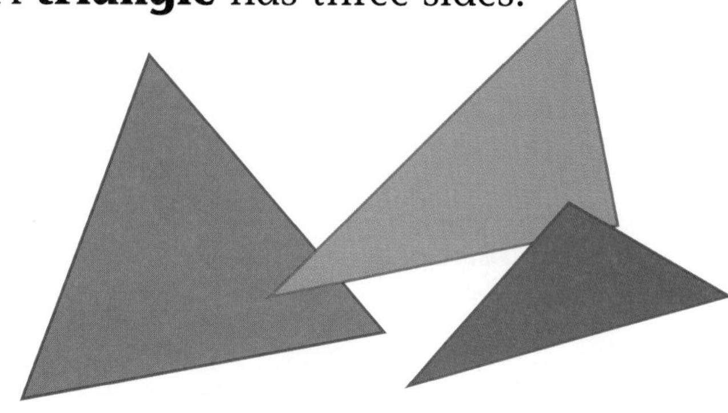

tunnel

This **tunnel** goes through the mountain.

type

You can use a computer to **type** a letter.

A B C D E F G H I J K L M N O P Q R S T U V W X Y Z

Uu

umbrella

You need your **umbrella** when it rains.

uncle

This is my favorite **uncle**! He is my father's brother.

underground

These foxes sleep **underground**.

underline

Please **underline** your name.

My name is <u>Jenna</u>.

understand

Please say that again.
I do not **understand**.

unhappy

This girl is **unhappy**.
She is not smiling.

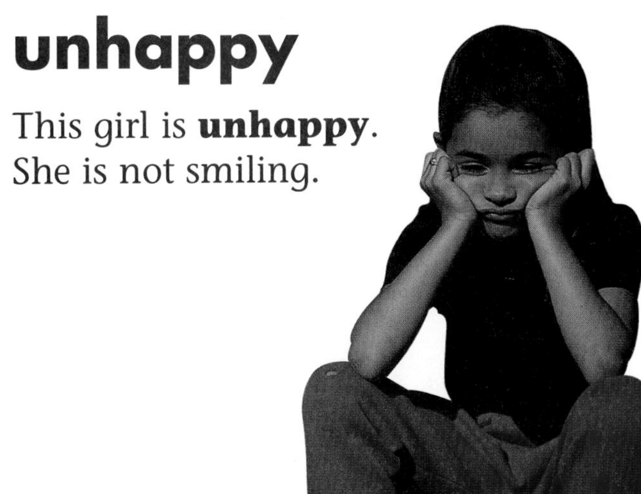

United States

The **United States** is a country. There are fifty states in the United States. The flag has one star for every state.

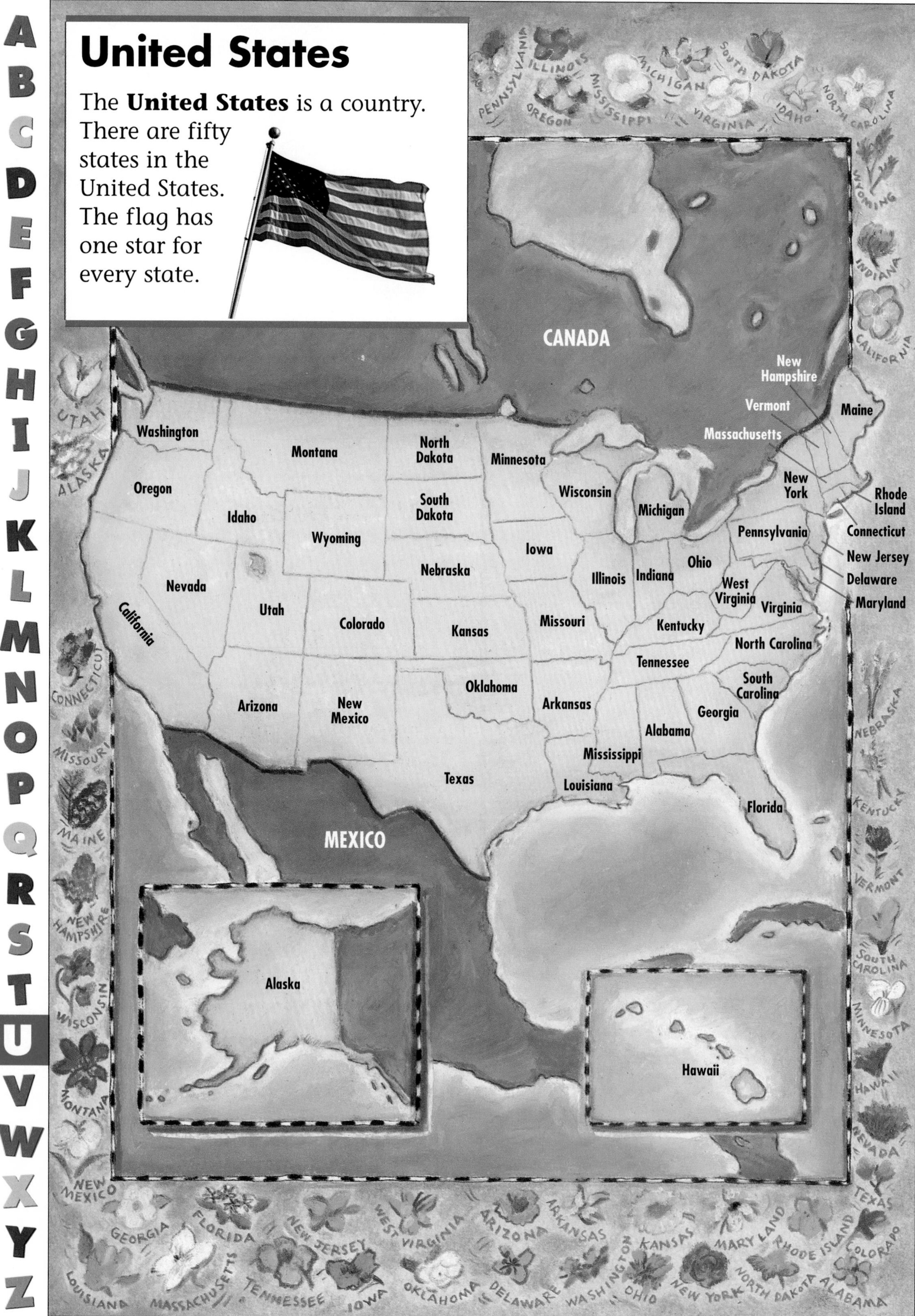

vase

You can put flowers in a **vase**.

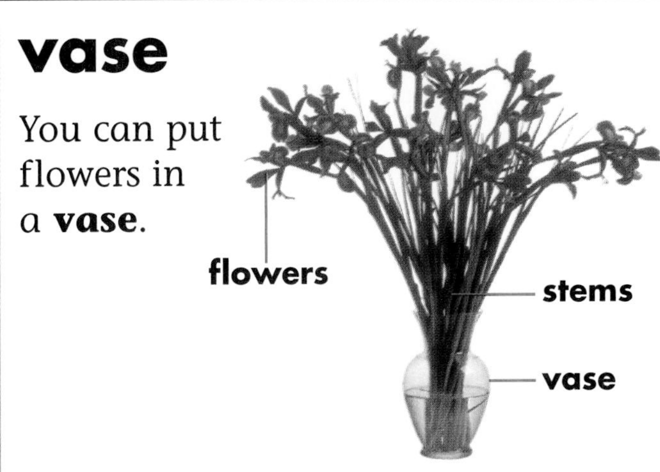

valentine

I give a **valentine** to my friend on February 14.

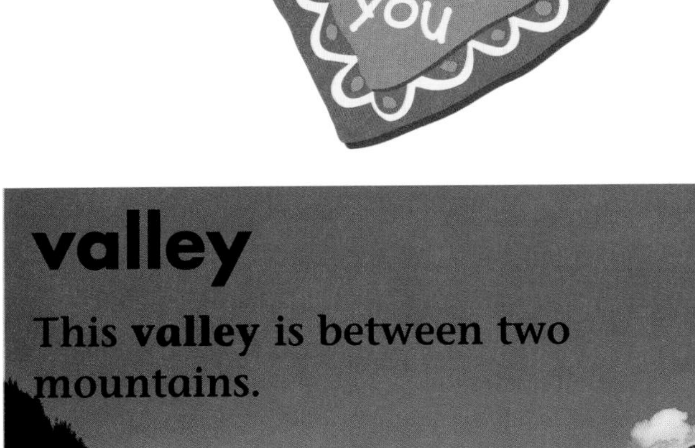

valley

This **valley** is between two mountains.

value

The **value** of this notebook is $1.99.

vegetable

A **vegetable** is a healthy food.

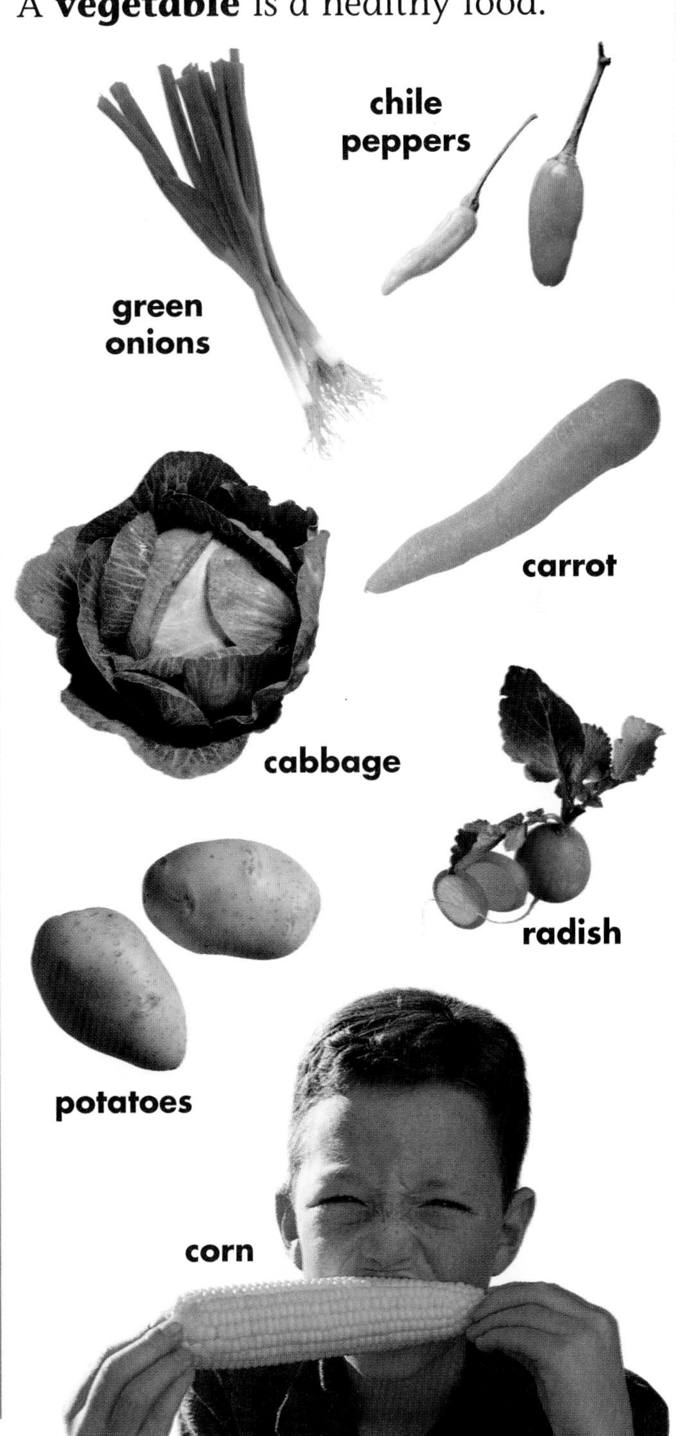

a b c d e f g h i j k l m n o p q r s t u v w x y z

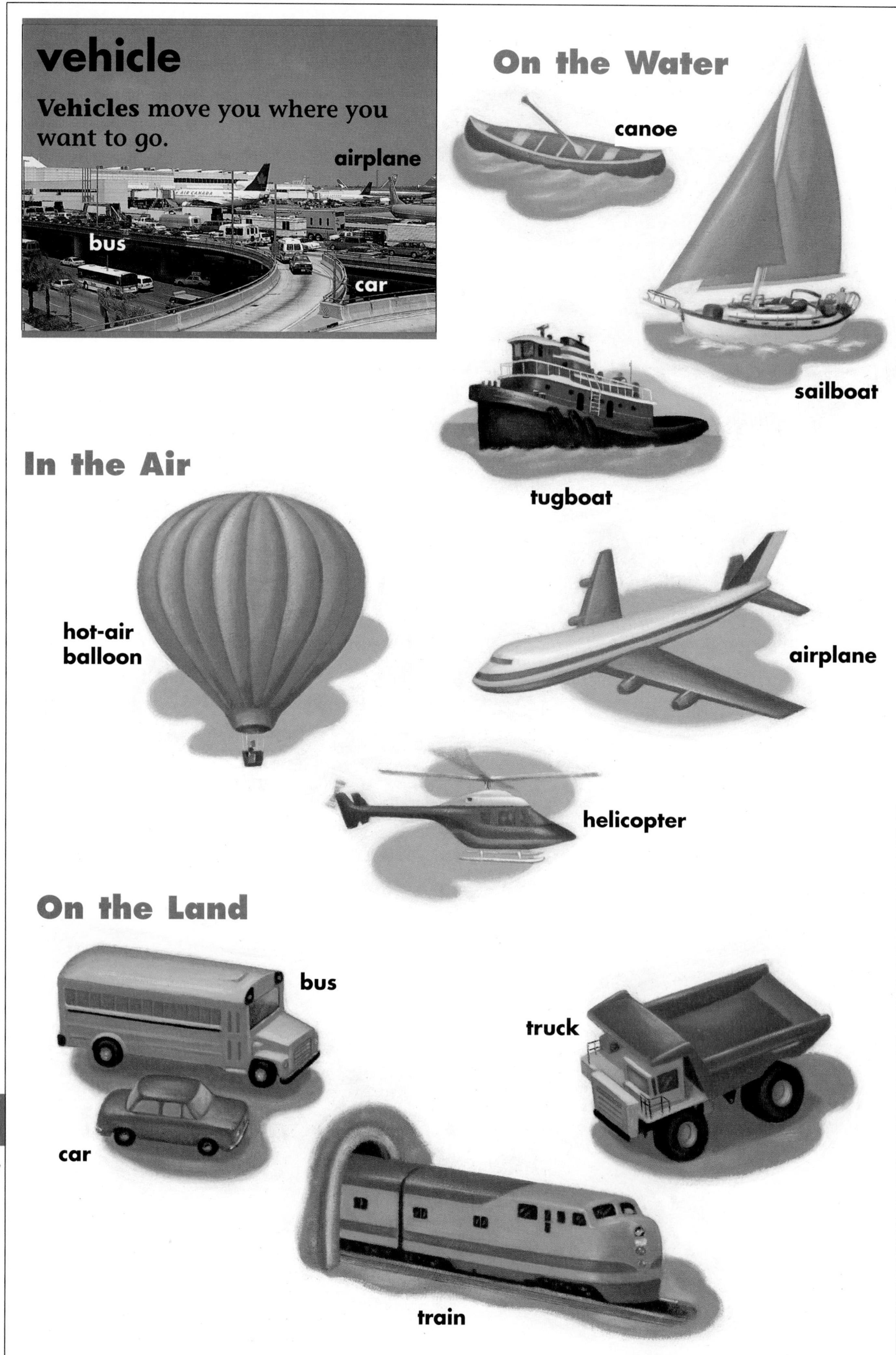
vehicle
Vehicles move you where you want to go.
airplane
bus
car
On the Water
canoe
sailboat
tugboat
In the Air
hot-air balloon
airplane
helicopter
On the Land
bus
truck
car
train

A
B
C
D
E
F
G
H
I
J
K
L
M
N
O
P
Q
R
S
T
U
V
W
X
Y
Z

Ww

waste

Don't **waste** water. Turn it off.

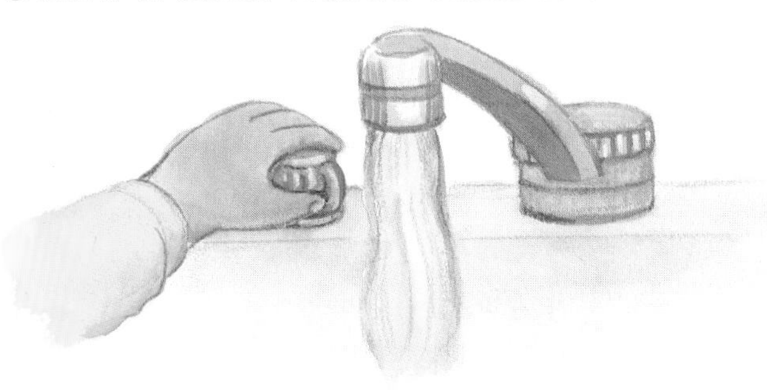

walk

Some people like to **walk** for exercise.

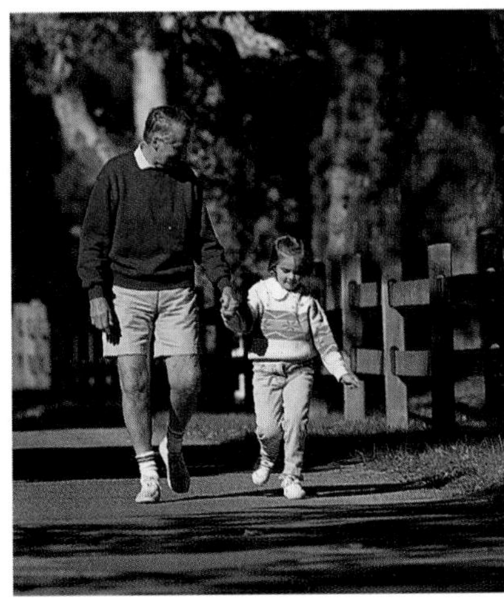

want

These children **want** some ice cream.

wash

You can **wash** your clothes in a washing machine.

watch

1. You can wear a **watch** on your wrist.

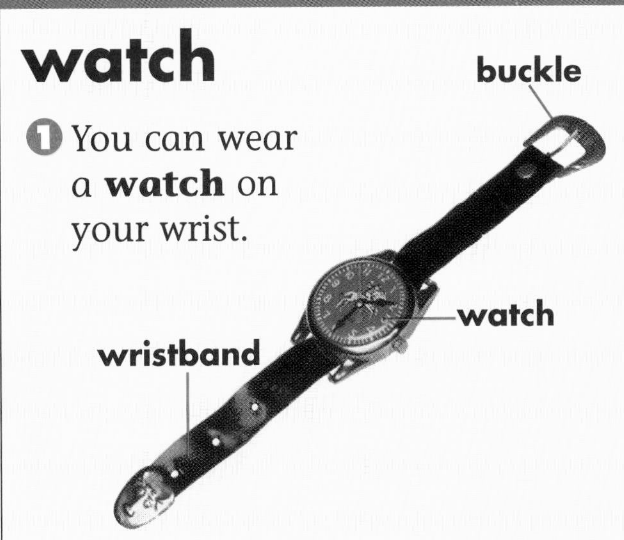

2. They like to **watch** birds.

water

You can find **water** in rivers, lakes, and oceans.

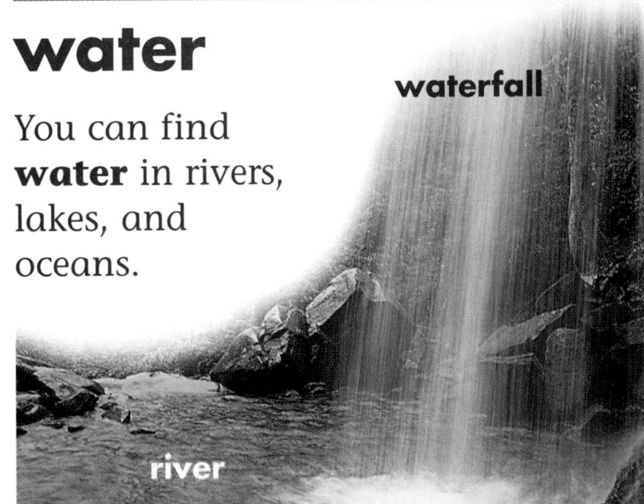

weather

The **weather** is always changing. We can feel the changes in the air.

a rainy day

gray sky

a snowy day

snowflakes

a stormy day

lightning
dark sky

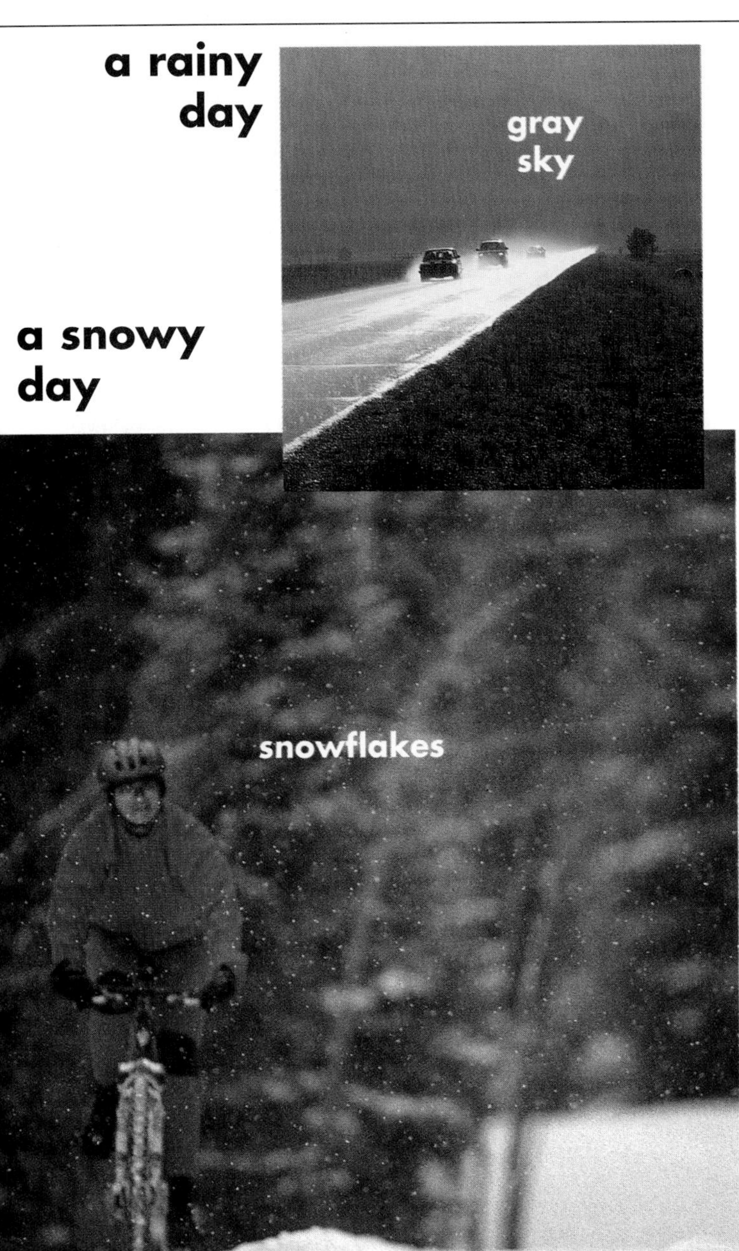

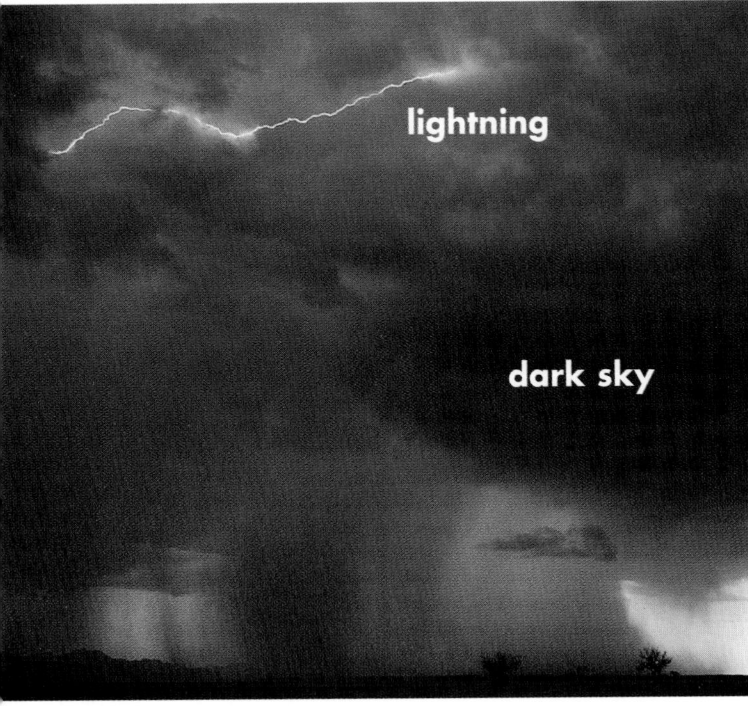

What will the weather be like?

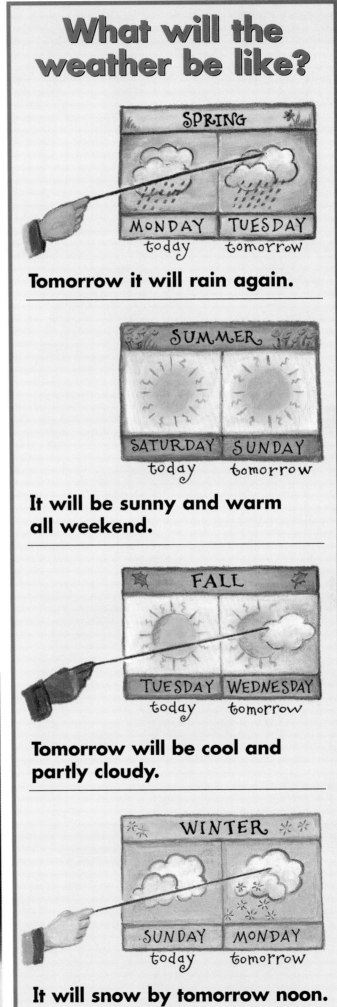

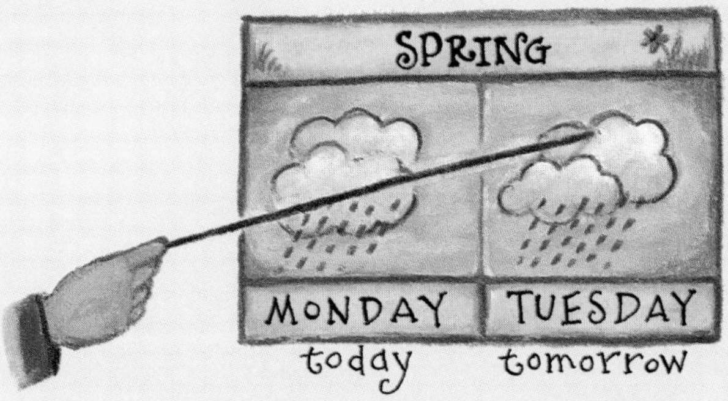

SPRING
MONDAY
TUESDAY
today
tomorrow

Tomorrow it will rain again.

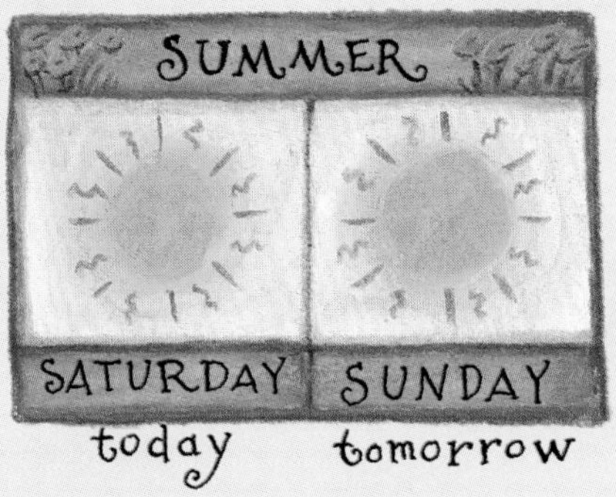

SUMMER
SATURDAY
SUNDAY
today
tomorrow

It will be sunny and warm all weekend.

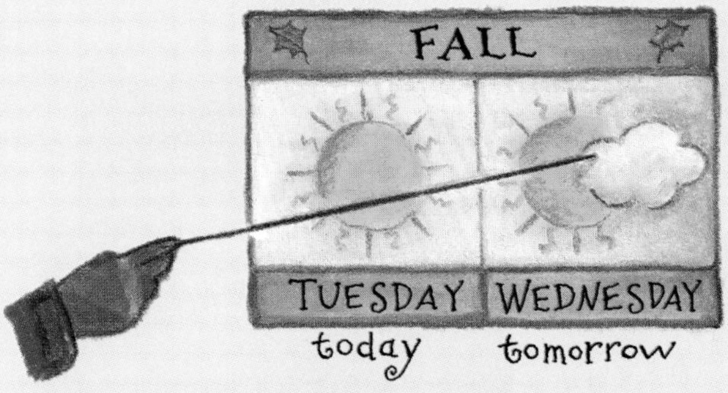

FALL
TUESDAY
WEDNESDAY
today
tomorrow

Tomorrow will be cool and partly cloudy.

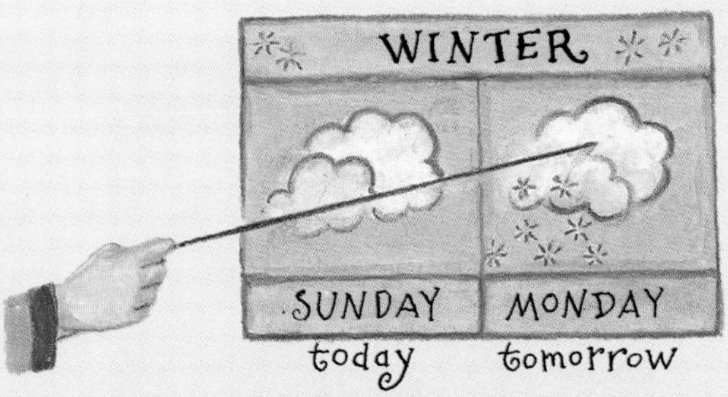

WINTER
SUNDAY
MONDAY
today
tomorrow

It will snow by tomorrow noon.

A B C D E F G H I J K L M N O P Q R S T U V **W** X Y Z

weigh

You can find out how much you **weigh** on a scale.

well

1 He is not **well**. He is sick.

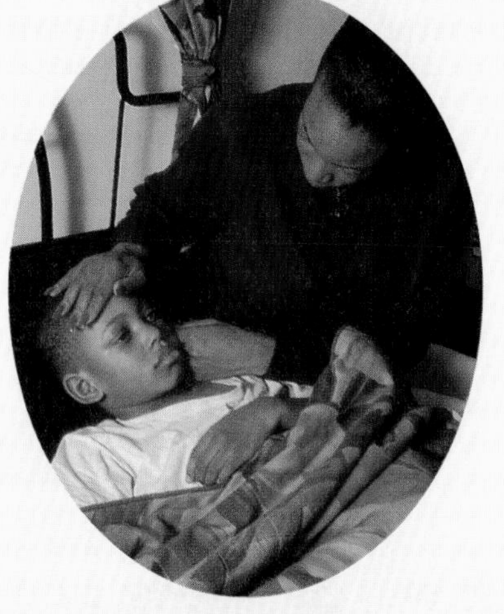

2 People can get water from a **well**.

wet

This pup is really **wet**!

wheel

A **wheel** rolls around and around.

whisper

Please **whisper**. We don't want to wake up the baby.

wild

Some animals are **wild**. They are not pets.

winner

Each **winner** gets a medal.

wise

You can learn a lot from the **wise** words of an author.

Julia Alvarez, author

woman

One **woman** holds her diploma while all the **women** smile.

world

This photograph of the **world** was taken from outer space.

write

She can **write** her name.

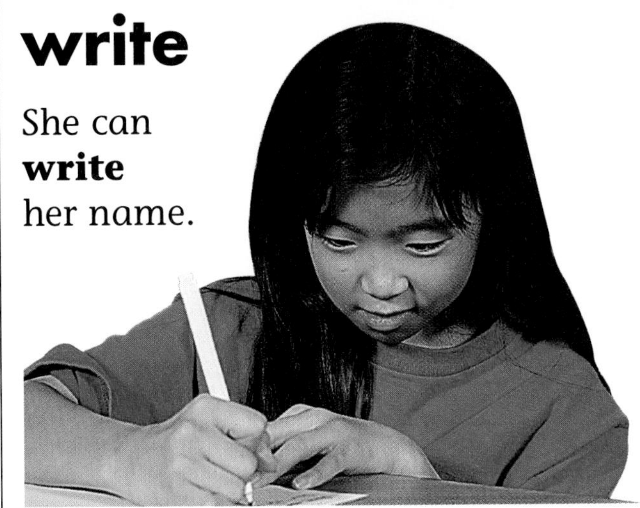

X-ray

An **X-ray** can show the bones inside your body.

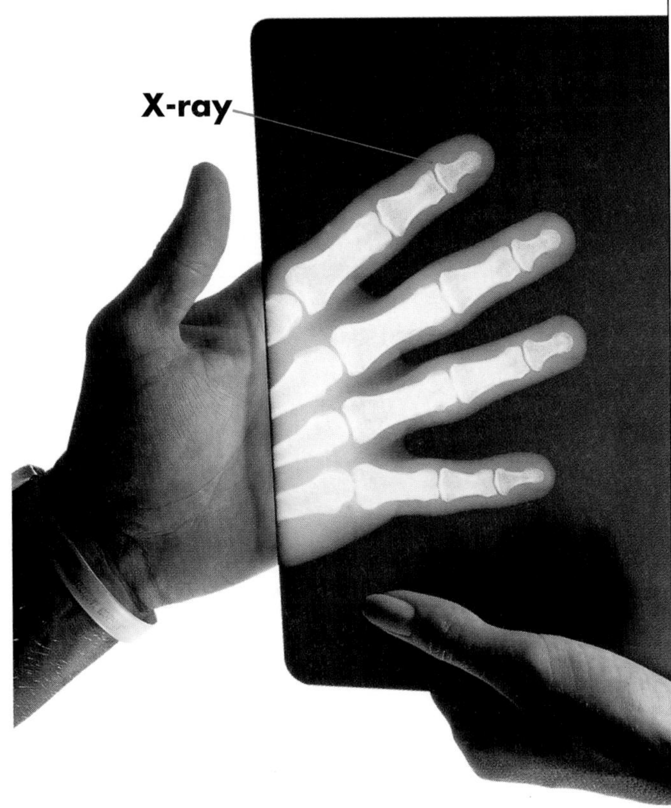

xylophone

It's fun to play music on a **xylophone**.

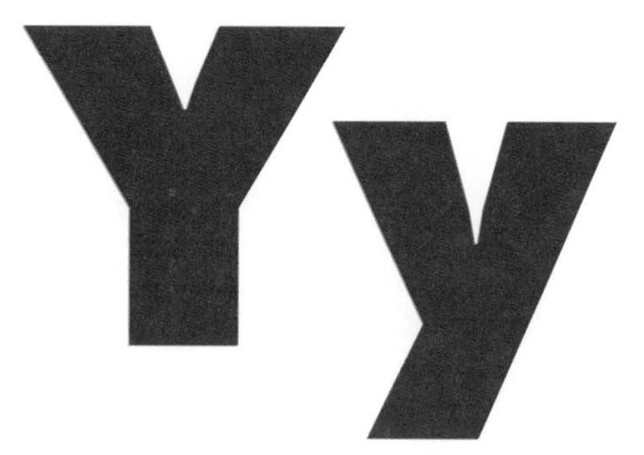

yard

This house has a big **yard**.

yarn

She spins **yarn** from wool.

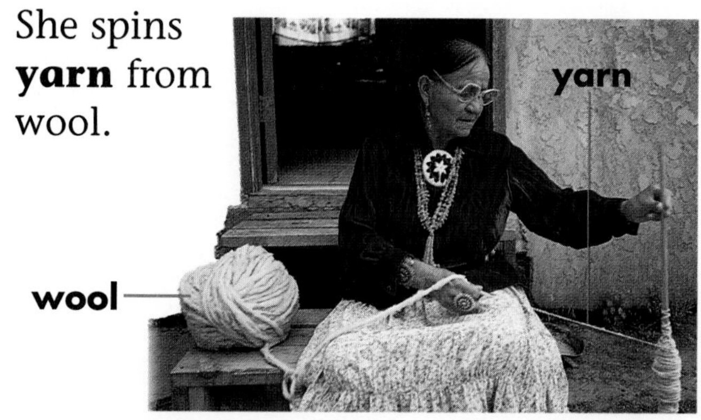

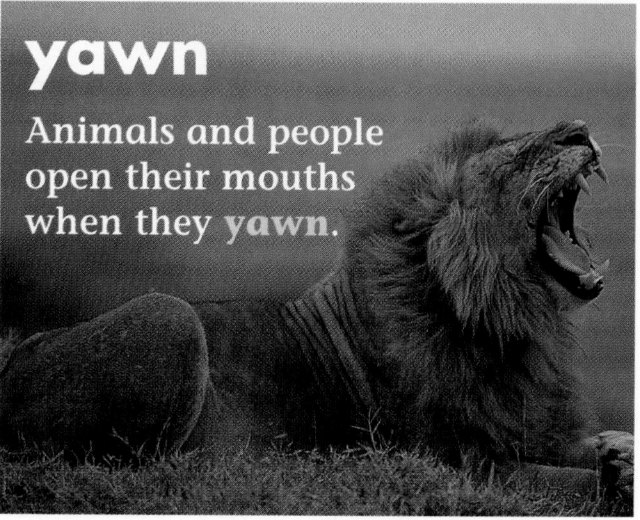

yawn

Animals and people open their mouths when they **yawn**.

year

A **year** has 12 months.

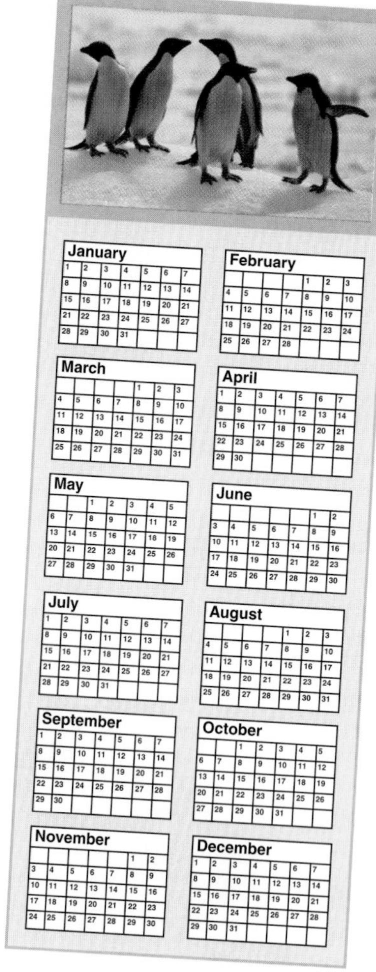

yell

Friends **yell** loudly at a game.

yes

Yes! I'm ready to go swimming!

yesterday

Today is Friday. **Yesterday** was Thursday.

Yesterday, I went to the zoo.

Last week, I saw a dragon dance.

Last month, I visited my uncle in Arizona.

Zz

zero

Write the number 1 and the number **zero** to make the number 10.

zip

She will **zip** up her coat.

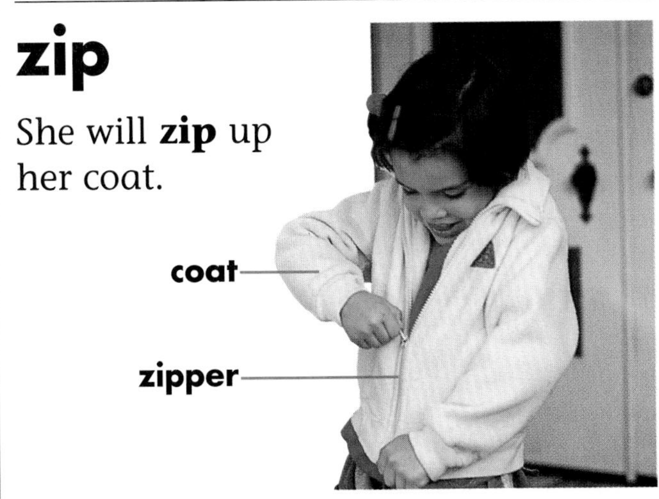

zipper

A **zipper** opens and closes.

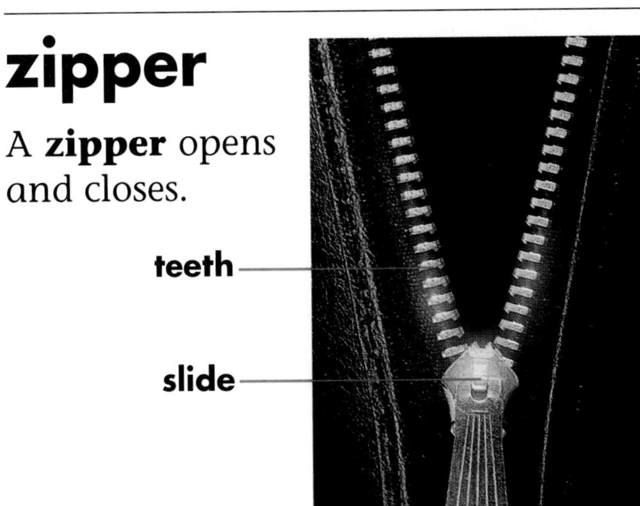

A
B
C
D
E
F
G
H
I
J
K
L
M
N
O
P
Q
R
S
T
U
V
W
X
Y
Z

ZOO

Many different animals live at the **zoo**. Let's visit them!

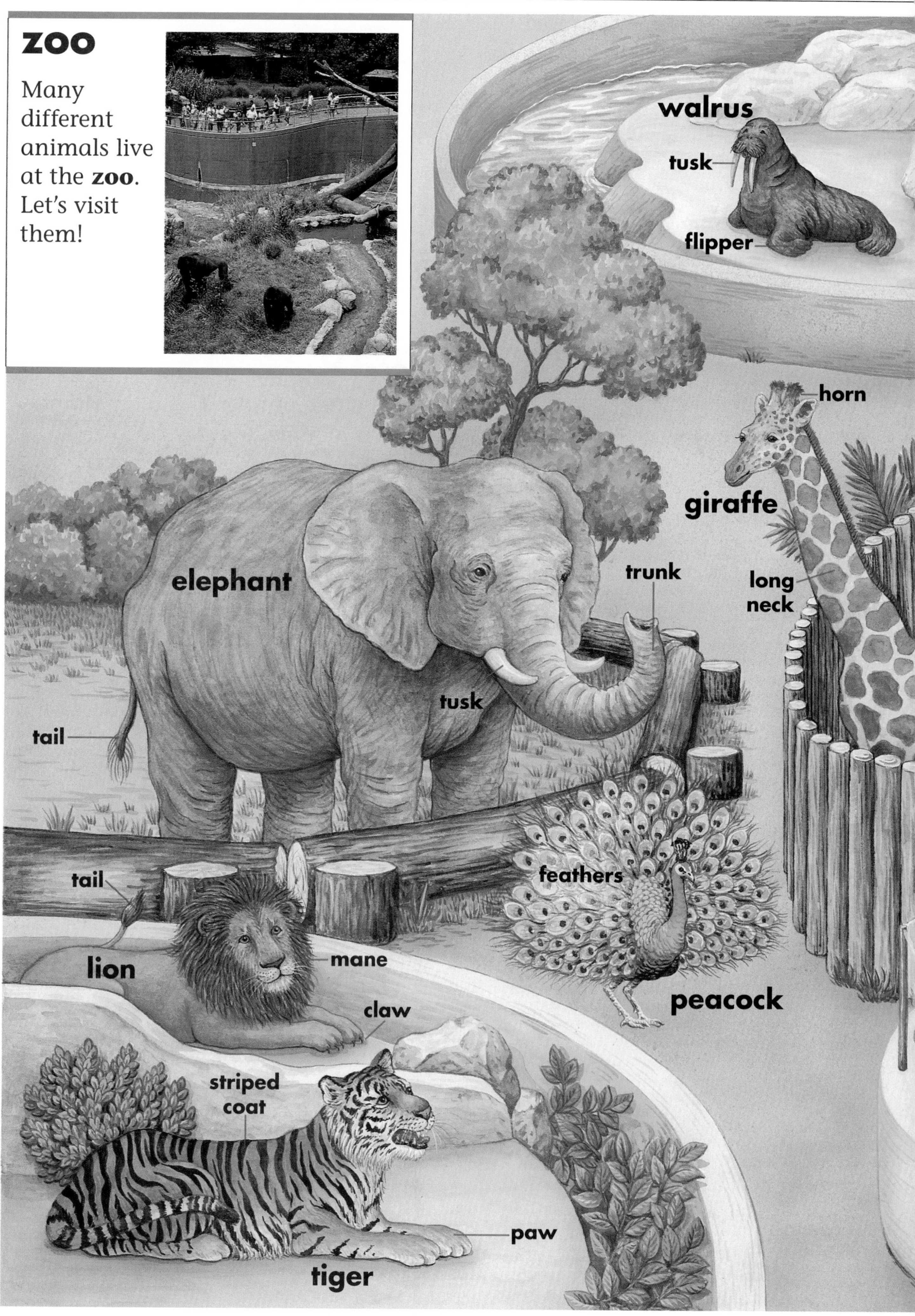

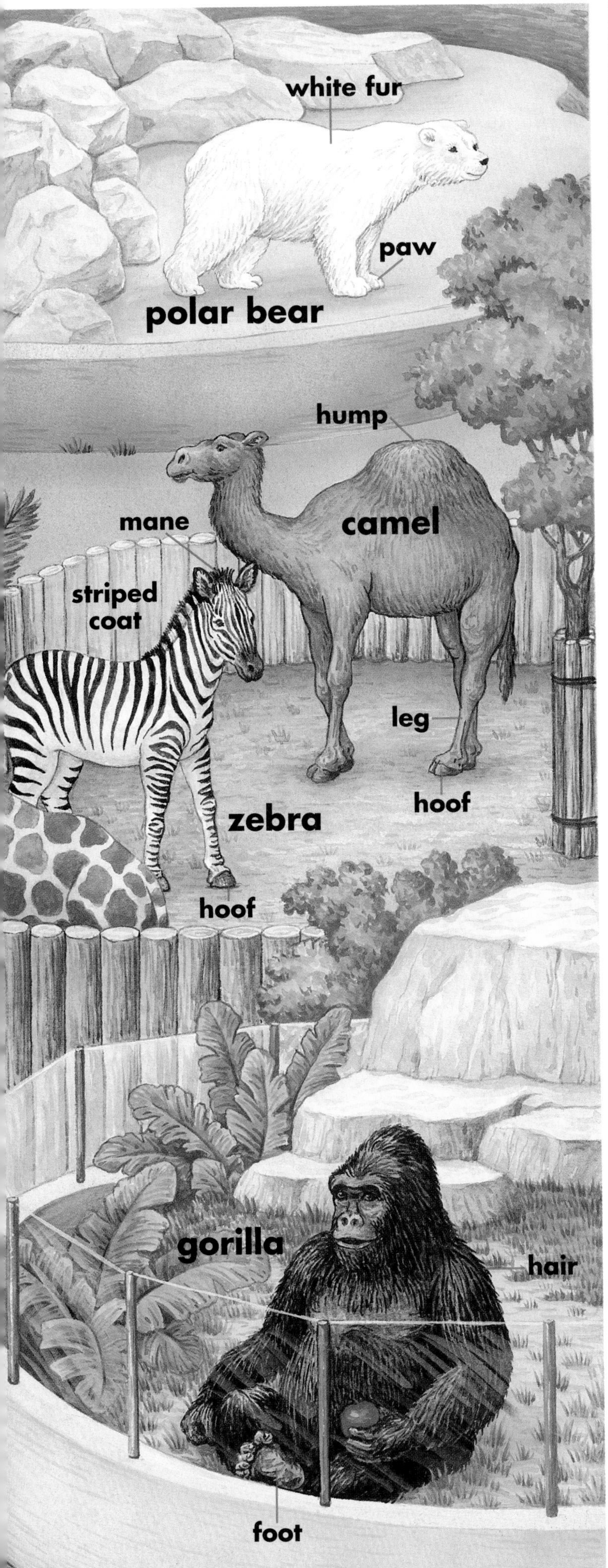

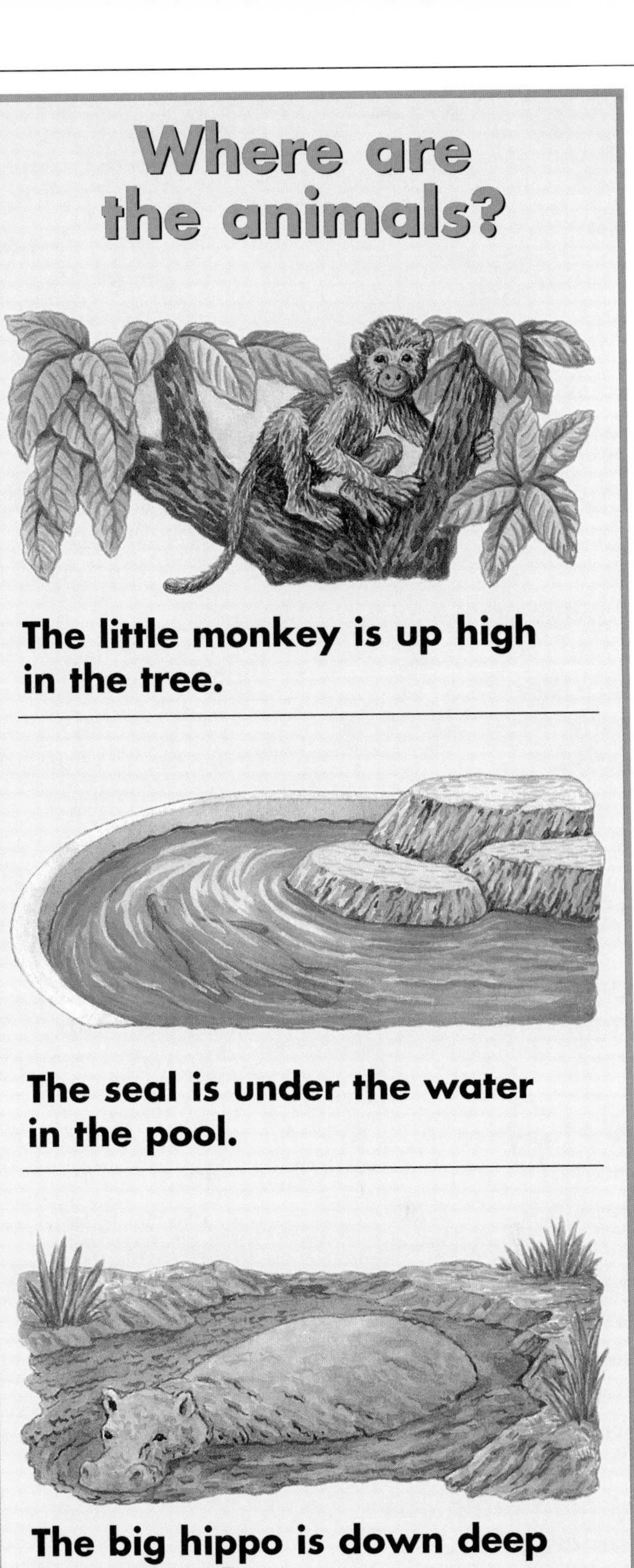

Where are the animals?

The little monkey is up high in the tree.

The seal is under the water in the pool.

The big hippo is down deep in the mud.

The panda is on the grass near the gate.

a b c d e f g h i j k l m n o p q r s t u v w x y z

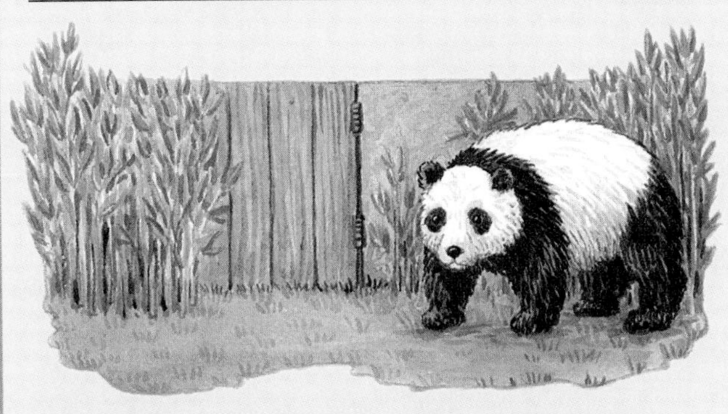

Word-Finder Index

Aa

abdomen . . . 8, 13
above . . . 66
add . . . 5
address . . . 5
adobe home . . . 44
adult . . . 5, 42
afternoon . . . 5
again . . . 105
age . . . 5, 68
age order . . . 68
air . . . 87, 102
air bladder . . . 75
air tank . . . 87
airplane . . . 102
Alabama . . . 100
alike . . . 5
all . . . 81
alphabet . . . 5
Alaska . . . 100
ambulance . . . 63
anemone . . . 86
angry . . . 36
animal . . . 6
animal families . . . 6
animals . . . 7, 27, 86, 87, 111
ankle . . . 13
ant . . . 8, 50
ant hill . . . 8
anteater . . . 50
antelope jack rabbit . . . 27
antelope squirrel . . . 27
antenna . . . 8, 48
apartment . . . 62
apartment buildings . . . 62
apartments . . . 44
apple . . . 8, 38, 51, 65
apple seed . . . 88
apples . . . 40
April . . . 16
architect . . . 19
Arizona . . . 100, 109
Arizona poppy . . . 26
Arkansas . . . 100
arm . . . 13, 95
armchair . . . 55
armor . . . 52
around . . . 8
asleep . . . 8
aster . . . 37
astronaut . . . 8
ate . . . 81
Atlantic Ocean . . . 23, 39
August . . . 16
author . . . 8, 107
avocado seed . . . 88
awake . . . 8

Bb

baby . . . 7, 9, 26, 42, 51, 72
baby kit foxes . . . 26
baby turtle . . . 7
back . . . 66
bag . . . 19
bagels . . . 40
baked goods . . . 40
bakery . . . 41
ball . . . 9, 20, 51, 71, 82, 95
balloon . . . 102
bamboo house . . . 44
banana . . . 38, 51, 65
bananas . . . 40
band . . . 9
• **bank** . . . 9, 82, 84
barber . . . 18, 63
barber shop . . . 63
bark . . . 83
barn . . . 34
barn swallow . . . 12
baseball . . . 9, 92
basket . . . 9, 56, 71
basketball . . . 9, 92
bass . . . 68
bat . . . 14, 39
bathing suit . . . 22
bathroom . . . 10
bathtub . . . 10
beach clothing . . . 22
beans . . . 40
bean stalk . . . 57
bear . . . 7, 37, 111
beat . . . 10
beautiful . . . 10
beaver-tail cactus . . . 27
bed . . . 10
bedroom . . . 10
bedspread . . . 10
bee . . . 48
beef . . . 40
beetle . . . 48
begin . . . 10
beginning . . . 10

Expanded entries appear **in color**.

•Indicates a multiple-meaning entry.

behind . . . 11
below . . . 66
belt . . . 18
bench . . . 39
berries . . . 75
beside . . . 11
between . . . 11
bicycle . . . 11
big . . . 11
bike . . . 52, 63, 71, 72, 76, 84
bike shop . . . 63
• bill . . . 11, 12, 81
bills . . . 60
bin . . . 17
bird . . . 6, 7, 12, 37, 73
birdhouse . . . 15
birds . . . 7
birthday . . . 12
bite . . . 12
blackboard . . . 83
blade . . . 75
blanket . . . 8
blocks . . . 56, 72
blow . . . 12
blowhole . . . 87
blue . . . 23, 104
blue sky . . . 104
blueprint . . . 19
boat . . . 29, 43, 83
boats . . . 37
bobcat . . . 26
body . . . 13
bongo . . . 50
book . . . 10, 14, 19, 47, 69
books . . . 54, 85
bookshelves . . . 85
boot . . . 22, 70
booth . . . 33
bottle . . . 44
bottled water . . . 41
bottom . . . 14
bow . . . 96
bowl . . . 14, 73
bowling . . . 82
bowling ball . . . 82
box . . . 14
boy . . . 14
branch . . . 75
Brazil . . . 24
bread . . . 9, 40, 41
break . . . 14
breathe . . . 87
bride . . . 58
bright . . . 14
bring . . . 14
broccoli . . . 35
brush . . . 17
bubble . . . 12
bucket . . . 21
buckle . . . 103
bud . . . 37
build . . . 15
building . . . 15, 21
buildings . . . 62
bulb . . . 31
burn . . . 15
burrow . . . 27
burrowing owl . . . 26
bus . . . 15, 18, 85, 102
busboy . . . 81
bus driver . . . 18
bush . . . 26, 75
butter . . . 40
butterfly . . . 48
butterfly life cycle . . . 48
button . . . 15
buy . . . 15

Cc

cab . . . 16
cabbage . . . 101
cabin . . . 44
cabinet . . . 10, 52
cactus . . . 26, 27
cactus wren . . . 26
cafeteria . . . 16
cage . . . 73
cages . . . 90
cake . . . 12, 20
cakes . . . 40
calculator . . . 16
calendar . . . 16, 96
calf . . . 6
California . . . 93, 100
call . . . 16
camel . . . 111
camels . . . 57
camp . . . 17
• can . . . 17, 61, 69, 71
Canada . . . 100
candle . . . 12, 15, 20
canned . . . 41
cannery . . . 41

canoe . . . 53, 102
canopy . . . 78
canopy layer . . . 78
cap . . . 11, 22
cape . . . 57
capital . . . 5, 17, 89, 93
capital letter . . . 5, 89
caps . . . 84
car . . . 17, 102
card . . . 17
care . . . 17
career . . . 18
careers . . . 18
cargo . . . 20, 78
carpenter . . . 15, 18
carrot . . . 101
carrots . . . 35, 40
cart . . . 81, 90
carton . . . 31
carton of eggs . . . 31
cashier . . . 80
castle . . . 57
cat . . . 6, 73
catch . . . 20
catching a ball . . . 71
caterpillar . . . 48
caught . . . 41
cause . . . 20, 30
celebration . . . 20
celery . . . 40
cello . . . 68
centerpiece . . . 81
cereal . . . 41
chain . . . 11
chair . . . 52, 81
chalk . . . 29
chalkboard . . . 85
• **change** . . . 20
character . . . 20
checking out . . . 19
cheek . . . 33
cheese . . . 40, 41
chest . . . 10, 13
chest of drawers . . . 10
chicken . . . 40
chicks . . . 6
child . . . 5, 20, 42, 70
children . . . 20
chile peppers . . . 101
chilies . . . 40
chimney . . . 45
chimpanzee . . . 57
chin . . . 33
chopsticks . . . 14
chrysalis . . . 48
circle . . . 21, 90
circus . . . 21
city . . . 21
city apartments . . . 44
clams . . . 40
classify . . . 21
classroom . . . 85
claw . . . 12, 79, 110
clay . . . 21
clay pot . . . 21
clean . . . 21, 66, 80
clean dishes . . . 80
climb . . . 21
clippers . . . 97
clock . . . 5, 96
closed . . . 67
closet . . . 96
cloth . . . 89
clothes . . . 69
clothing . . . 22
cloud . . . 58, 104
clouds . . . 92
cloudy . . . 104, 105
cloudy day . . . 104
clown . . . 38
clown fish . . . 86
coat . . . 109, 110
coffee shop . . . 62
coffee table . . . 55
coins . . . 60, 84
cold . . . 67
collar . . . 61
collarbone . . . 91
collared lizard . . . 26
color . . . 23
Colorado . . . 100
comb . . . 18
come . . . 23, 41, 87
compare . . . 23
compass . . . 19
compass rose . . . 58
computer . . . 23, 47
conductor . . . 68
cone . . . 21
Connecticut . . . 100
construction worker . . . 19
continent . . . 23
cook . . . 19, 23, 81
cookies . . . 14, 40
cool . . . 105
coral . . . 86

cord . . . 31
core . . . 8
corn . . . 35, 101
corner . . . 79
costume . . . 20
cottage . . . 44
couch . . . 55
count . . . 23
counter . . . 52
• **country** . . . 24
cousin . . . 24
cover . . . 14
cow . . . 6, 34
coyote . . . 26
crab . . . 88
crackers . . . 41
crawl . . . 27
crayon . . . 32
cream . . . 40
creosote bush . . . 26
crocodile . . . 50, 79
crops . . . 35
cross . . . 63
crosswalk . . . 62, 63
cube . . . 21, 24
cubs . . . 7
cucumbers . . . 35
cup . . . 36, 59
cups . . . 97
curly . . . 24
curly hair . . . 24
curtains . . . 55
curved line . . . 55
customer . . . 24, 80
cut . . . 24
cylinder . . . 21, 24

Dd

dairy foods . . . 40
daisy . . . 37
dance . . . 25, 109
dandelion seed . . . 88
dangerous . . . 25
dark . . . 25, 105
dark sky . . . 105
daughter . . . 25, 33
day . . . 25, 104, 105
days of the week . . . 16
December . . . 16
decorate . . . 25
decorations . . . 25
deep . . . 25, 111
deer . . . 7, 27, 37
Delaware . . . 100
deli counter . . . 41
den . . . 7, 99
desert . . . 26, 27
desert king snake . . . 27
desert marigold . . . 27
desk . . . 65, 85
dessert . . . 81
dessert cart . . . 81
details . . . 70
diamond . . . 28
diamond shape . . . 28
difference . . . 28
different . . . 28
dig . . . 28
dime . . . 60, 90
dining room . . . 80
dinner . . . 28, 81
diploma . . . 107
• **directions** . . . 28
dirt . . . 25
dirty . . . 66, 81
dirty dishes . . . 81
dish . . . 64
dishes . . . 80, 81
dishwasher . . . 80
display screen . . . 16
diver . . . 87
divide . . . 28
do . . . 29
dock . . . 29
doctor . . . 18
dog . . . 6, 73
dollar . . . 60
dollars . . . 60
dolphins . . . 57
donkey . . . 34
door . . . 17, 45
dots . . . 74
double . . . 29
down . . . 66
dragon . . . 57, 70, 109
dragonfly . . . 48
draw . . . 29
drawers . . . 10
drink . . . 29, 71
drinking fountain . . . 71
driver . . . 16, 18
driving . . . 19
drop . . . 29
drum . . . 9, 10, 68
dry . . . 29

duck . . . 12, 34
ducks . . . 71
dump truck . . . 19
dumpster . . . 39
dust . . . 29
duster . . . 29
dusty . . . 29

Ee

each . . . 30
eagle . . . 12
ear . . . 13, 89
early . . . 30
earn . . . 30
easel . . . 36
easy . . . 30
eat . . . 30
eating . . . 71
edge . . . 30
eel . . . 88
effect . . . 30
egg . . . 31, 48
eggs . . . 31, 40
eight . . . 64
eighty . . . 64
elbow . . . 13, 76
elbow pad . . . 76
elder . . . 42
electrical outlet . . . 31
electricity . . . 31
elephant . . . 50, 110
elevator . . . 31
elf owl . . . 27
emergent layer . . . 78
empty . . . 66
• end . . . 31
energy . . . 31
enjoy . . . 31
enter . . . 32
envelope . . . 5
equal . . . 32
eraser . . . 31, 83, 97
even . . . 32
even numbers . . . 32
every . . . 32
exclamation mark . . . 77
exercise . . . 32
exercise wheel . . . 73
exit . . . 32
experiment . . . 32
eye . . . 33, 89
eyebrow . . . 33

Ff

face . . . 33, 58
factory . . . 33
Fahrenheit . . . 33
• fair . . . 33
fairy godmother . . . 57
fall . . . 88, 105
family . . . 33, 81
families . . . 6
fan . . . 81
farm . . . 34, 35, 41
farm animals . . . 34
farmer . . . 35
father . . . 25, 33, 70, 99
faucet . . . 74
feather . . . 29
feather duster . . . 29
featherduster worm . . . 87
feathers . . . 12, 110
February . . . 16
feeding the ducks . . . 71
feelings . . . 36
fence . . . 44, 45
fern . . . 75
ferns . . . 50
Ferris wheel . . . 33
field . . . 35
fifty . . . 64
fill . . . 36
fin . . . 36, 87
find . . . 36
finger . . . 13
finish . . . 36, 78
finish line . . . 78
fire . . . 16
fire station . . . 62
fire truck . . . 19, 62
firefighter . . . 19
first . . . 53, 94
fish . . . 36, 40, 41, 73, 86, 87
fish bowl . . . 73
fishermen . . . 41
five . . . 60, 64
five dollars . . . 60
fix . . . 36
fixing . . . 19
flag . . . 37
flagpole . . . 37
flags . . . 70
flame . . . 15
flipper . . . 110
float . . . 37

floor . . . 78
Florida . . . 17, 100
flower . . . 37, 61
flower store . . . 62
flowers . . . 58, 101
flute . . . 68
fly . . . 37
folder . . . 51
food . . . 35, 37, 41
foods . . . 40, 41
foot . . . 12, 13, 51, 111
football . . . 9, 92
forehead . . . 33
forest . . . 37, 78
forest floor . . . 78
forget . . . 38
fork . . . 97
forty . . . 64
forward . . . 38
fountain . . . 71
four . . . 64
fox . . . 7
foxes . . . 7, 26
fraction . . . 38
frame . . . 74
free . . . 38
fried . . . 31
fried egg . . . 31
friend . . . 38
frog . . . 7, 20
frogs . . . 7
fronds . . . 75
front . . . 66, 83
front row . . . 83
frozen foods . . . 41
fruit . . . 38, 40
fruit store . . . 62
full . . . 66
funny . . . 38
fur . . . 111

Gg

game . . . 28
garbage . . . 39
garden . . . 39, 97
gate . . . 111
gavel . . . 49
Georgia . . . 100
get . . . 39
getting a drink . . . 71
giant . . . 57
gift . . . 12
gill . . . 87
giraffe . . . 110
girl . . . 39
give . . . 39
glass . . . 30, 36, 46, 81
glasses . . . 88
globe . . . 39
glove . . . 20
glue . . . 36
go . . . 39
goat . . . 6, 34
goldfish . . . 73
gorilla . . . 111
grandfather . . . 33
grandmother . . . 33
grape . . . 38
grapes . . . 40, 41, 65
grass . . . 75, 111
grass roof . . . 44
grasshopper . . . 48
gray . . . 105
gray sky . . . 105
great-grandmother . . . 33
green . . . 23
green beans . . . 40
green lime . . . 23
green onions . . . 101
grew . . . 41
grocery . . . 40, 41
groom . . . 58
ground . . . 27, 42, 83
ground beef . . . 40
grow . . . 42
guard . . . 42
guess . . . 42
guide . . . 42
guinea pig . . . 73
guitar . . . 9

Hh

hair . . . 13, 24, 111
half . . . 43
ham . . . 41
hammer . . . 15, 97
hamster . . . 61, 73
hand . . . 54, 96
handle . . . 9
handlebars . . . 11
happy . . . 36
harbor . . . 43
hard . . . 66
hard hat . . . 18

hardwood tree 50
harvest 35
hat 12, 18, 22
have 43
Hawaii 100
hawk 46
head 8
headlight 17, 90
headline 64
hear 89
heart 43
heavy 66
height 59
helicopter 102
helmet 52, 72, 76, 84
help 43
hen 6
hide 44
high 111
high chair 80
hill 44
hippo 111
hippopotamus 50
hoe 97
hold 44
hole 7
holiday 44
home 44
hood 17, 57
hoof 111
hopscotch squares 38
horn 110
hornbill 50
horny scales 79
horse 34
hose 106
hospital 63
hostess 80
hot 67
hot-air balloon 102
hour 96
hour hand 96
house 19, 44, 45, 108
houseboat 44
howl 46
hug 46
huge 46
hummingbird 12
hump 111
hundred 64
hungry 46
hunt 46
hurry 46
hurt 46
husband 46

Ii

ice 47
ice cream 41
ice skate 47
Idaho 100
idea 47, 70
ill 47
Illinois 100
imagine 47
include 47
indent 70
Indiana 100
information 47
insect 48, 96
inside 67
interesting 48
international 48
invitation 48
Iowa 100
island 48

Jj

jack rabbit 27
jack-in-the-box 94
jacket 22, 77
January 16
jar 49
jaw 91
jellyfish 87
job 49
joey 7
jogging 71
join 49
journey 49
judge 49
juice 41, 49
juice bars 41
July 16
jump 49
jump rope 46, 49
jumping rope 71
June 16
jungle 50

Kk

kangaroo 7
kangaroo rat 27

Kansas . . . 100
keep . . . 51
Kentucky . . . 100
kettle . . . 97
key . . . 16, 51, 58
keyboard . . . 23, 60, 74
kick . . . 51
kid . . . 6
kimono . . . 91
kind . . . 51
kiss . . . 51
kitchen . . . 52, 81, 97
kite . . . 52
kittens . . . 6
kiwi . . . 38
knee . . . 13, 46, 76
kneecap . . . 91
knee pad . . . 76
knife . . . 52, 97
knight . . . 52
knock . . . 52
knot . . . 52
know . . . 52

Ll

ladder . . . 19
ladybug . . . 48
lake . . . 53
lamb . . . 6
lamp . . . 10, 55
land . . . 53, 86, 102
landing gear . . . 53
lane . . . 82
language . . . 53
large . . . 67
largest . . . 68
last . . . 53
last week . . . 109
late . . . 53
laugh . . . 53
laundry . . . 56
laundry basket . . . 56
layer . . . 78
lead . . . 31
leaf . . . 37, 75
leafcutter ant . . . 50
learn . . . 54
least . . . 54
leave . . . 54
leaves . . . 75, 98
left . . . 54
left hand . . . 54
leg . . . 8, 13, 48, 92, 111
lemon . . . 23
lemons . . . 40
length . . . 59
leopard . . . 50
less . . . 54
lesson . . . 54
letter . . . 5, 54, 56, 89
letter carrier . . . 19
letters . . . 19
lettuce . . . 35, 40
librarian . . . 19
library . . . 54, 85
library card . . . 19
lid . . . 49
life cycle . . . 48
lift . . . 55
light . . . 31, 55, 64, 66
light bulb . . . 31
lightning . . . 105
lily . . . 37
lime . . . 23
line . . . 55, 78
lion . . . 110
lion fish . . . 86
litter . . . 55
little . . . 11
live . . . 7, 55
living room . . . 55
lizard . . . 26, 79
loaves . . . 41
lock . . . 51
locker . . . 76
locomotive . . . 78
log cabin . . . 44
logs . . . 76
long . . . 12, 67, 79
long bill . . . 12
long neck . . . 110
long side . . . 79
Louisiana . . . 100
lowercase . . . 5
lowercase letter . . . 5
lunch . . . 38, 55
lunch box . . . 54
lungs . . . 87

Mm

machine . . . 35, 56
magic wand . . . 57
magnet . . . 32, 56
mail . . . 56

mail bag 19
mailbox 45, 56, 63
main 56
main idea 70
Maine 100
make 56
make-believe 57
mammal 57
man 57
mane 110, 111
map 42, 58
maple tree 88
maple tree seed 88
March 16
march 58
marigold 27
market 58
marry 58
Maryland 100
mask 58
Massachusetts 100
match 58
May 16
maybe 58
meadow 60
measure 59
measuring 59
measuring cup 59
measuring cups 97
measuring height and weight . . . 59
measuring length 59
measuring spoons 59
measuring volume 59
meat 40
medal 106
melons 40
men 57
menu 80
mesquite 26
Mexico 61, 100
Mexico City 61
Michigan 100
microphone 18
middle 60
milk 14, 40
milkweed 88
milkweed seed 88
Minnesota 100
mints 80
minus key 16
minute 96
minute hand 96
mirror 17
Missouri 100
mitten 22
mittens 77
money 60, 92
monkey 50, 111
Montana 100
month 16, 109
moon 14, 60
moose 37
more 60
morning 60
moss 50
most 60
mother 25, 33, 51, 70
mountain 60, 101
mouse 23, 26, 46
mouth 33
movie theater 62, 63
mud 111
mud nest 12
muffins 40
mule deer 27
music 60, 74
mussels 40

Nn

nail 15
name 5, 61, 98
napkin 46, 81
napkins 41
narrow 61
nation 61
nature 61
Nebraska 100
necessary 61
neck 13, 110
need 61
needle 89
neighbor 61
neighborhood 62, 63
nest 7, 12, 50
Nevada 100
new 67
New Hampshire 100
New Jersey 100
New Mexico 100
New York 100
newspaper 64
nickel 60
night 25, 64
nine 64
ninety 64

noodles . . . 41
North America . . . 39
North Carolina . . . 100
North Dakota . . . 100
nose . . . 33, 89
not . . . 64
notebook . . . 101
nothing . . . 64
November . . . 16
now . . . 64
number . . . 24, 64
number cube . . . 24
number word . . . 64
numbers . . . 32

Oo

oar . . . 83
observe . . . 65
ocean . . . 23, 39, 43, 65, 93
October . . . 16
off . . . 67
office . . . 65
often . . . 65
Ohio . . . 100
oil . . . 65
Oklahoma . . . 100
old . . . 67
oldest . . . 68
olives . . . 41
on . . . 67
one . . . 60, 64, 109
one dollar . . . 60
one hundred . . . 64
one month . . . 16
one thousand . . . 64
one week . . . 16
onions . . . 40, 101
• open . . . 65, 67
opposite . . . 66
orange . . . 23, 51
oranges . . . 40
orchestra . . . 68
orchid . . . 50
order . . . 68
Oregon . . . 100
outdoor clothing . . . 22
outlet . . . 31
outside . . . 67
oven . . . 52
over . . . 67
owl . . . 27
ox . . . 34

Pp

Pacific Ocean . . . 23, 93
• pack . . . 69
packaged food . . . 41
pad . . . 76
page . . . 69
paid . . . 81
pail . . . 69
pain . . . 69
• paint . . . 69
paint can . . . 69
paintbrush . . . 19, 36, 69, 97
painter . . . 19, 69
painting . . . 19, 42
paints . . . 36
pair . . . 70
palm trees . . . 82
panda . . . 111
pans . . . 81
pants . . . 22, 96
paper . . . 24, 70
paper clip . . . 56
paper clips . . . 32
papers . . . 51
parade . . . 70
paragraph . . . 70
parent . . . 70
parents . . . 70
park . . . 63, 71
parrot . . . 50
part . . . 72
partly . . . 105
party . . . 72
party hat . . . 12
passenger . . . 16
past . . . 72
path . . . 71, 72
pattern . . . 72
paw . . . 110, 111
pay . . . 72
peach . . . 38
peaches . . . 35
peacock . . . 110
peas . . . 41
pedal . . . 11
pelican . . . 86, 88
pen . . . 32, 97
pencil . . . 31, 32, 97
pencil sharpener . . . 97
pennies . . . 49
Pennsylvania . . . 100
penny . . . 60

people 21, 72
peppers 101
period 72, 89
person 72
pet 73
pet shop 63
petal 37
phone 74
photo 64
piano 54, 60, 74
pickles 41
picnic 71
picnic basket 71
picture 14, 74
piece 74
pies 40
pig 34
pile 74
pillow 10
pilot 18
pin 75
piñata 14
pipe 19, 74
pitcher 14
pizza 41
plain 74
plains 74
plane 53
plant 55, 75, 83
plants 27, 35, 86
plate 46
plates 49
play clothing 22
playground 85
plow 35
plows 35
plumber 19
plus key 16
pocket mouse 26
poem 75
point 75
polar bear 111
pole 37
polka dots 74
pollution 75
pond 7, 71
pony 17
pool 88, 94, 111
popcorn 65, 84
poppy 26
porcupine 26
pork 40
post office 63
postcard 89
pot 19, 21, 65
potato 41
potato salad 41
potatoes 40, 101
pots 81
practice 76
price 90
price tag 90
prickly pear cactus 26
prince 57
product 58, 76
product map 58
protect 76
pull 76
pup 7, 106
puppet 76
puppies 6
purple 23
push 76
push pin 75
put 76
puzzle 76
puzzled 36
python 50

Qq

quarter 32, 60
question 77
question mark 77
quickly 77
quiet 77
quilt 77
quite 77

Rr

rabbit 27, 37, 73
race 78
racetrack 78
radio 78
radishes 40, 101
railroad 78
railroad tracks 78
rain 78
rain forest 78
rainbow 10, 78
rainy 105
rainy day 105
raise 79
rake 97
rakes 61

rat . . . 27
rectangle . . . 79
recycle . . . 79
recycle bin . . . 17
red . . . 23
Red Riding Hood . . . 57
refrigerator . . . 52
remember . . . 79
reporter . . . 18
reptile . . . 79
restaurant . . . 80, 81
return . . . 82
Rhode Island . . . 100
rhyming . . . 75
rhyming words . . . 75
rib cage . . . 91
ribbon . . . 12
rice . . . 41
ride . . . 82
riding a bike . . . 71
• **right** . . . 82
river . . . 82, 103
river bank . . . 82
road . . . 90
roadrunner . . . 26
roast beef . . . 41
robe . . . 49
rock . . . 82, 88
• **roll** . . . 55, 82
roof . . . 17, 44, 45
room . . . 55
root . . . 83
rope . . . 46, 49, 71, 94
rose . . . 37, 58
rough . . . 83
• **row** . . . 83
rug . . . 10
rule . . . 83
ruler . . . 19, 59, 83, 97
run . . . 83
runway . . . 53
rush . . . 83

Ss

sack . . . 84
sad . . . 36
safe . . . 84
safety pin . . . 75
sage brush . . . 26
saguaro cactus . . . 26
sail . . . 84
sailboat . . . 84, 102
salad . . . 41
sale . . . 84
salt . . . 84
same . . . 84
sand . . . 15, 27, 69, 88
sand castle . . . 15
sandals . . . 108
sandbox . . . 71
sandpiper . . . 88
sandwiches . . . 41
sausage . . . 40
save . . . 84
saw . . . 15, 97, 109
say . . . 85
scale . . . 59, 85, 106
scales . . . 36, 79
scaly . . . 79
scaly skin . . . 79
scare . . . 85
scarf . . . 22, 77
scene . . . 85
school . . . 85, 97
school clothing . . . 22
school of fish . . . 86
scissors . . . 24, 97
scrape . . . 46
screen . . . 16, 23
screwdriver . . . 97
sea . . . 41, 48, 86, 87, 88
sea anemone . . . 86
sea horse . . . 87
sea lion . . . 88
sea star . . . 86
seal . . . 111
seals . . . 57, 87
seashore . . . 88
seasons . . . 88
seat . . . 11, 94
seaweed . . . 75, 87, 88
second . . . 94, 96
second hand . . . 96
secret . . . 88
secretary . . . 65
see . . . 88, 89
seed . . . 8, 88
seeds . . . 35
sell . . . 88
sells . . . 35
send . . . 89
senses . . . 89
sentence . . . 72, 89
September . . . 16
seven . . . 64

seventy 64
several 89
sew 89
sewing 56
sewing machine 56
shadow 89
shape 28, 90
shark 87
sharpener 97
sheep 6
sheet music 60, 74
shell 79
shine 90
shiny 90
ship 20, 43, 90
shirt 22
shoe store 62
shoelaces 28
shoes 22
shop 62, 63, 90
shopping 90
shopping cart 90
short 67, 79
short side 79
shorts 22
shoulder 13
shout 90
shovel 15, 69, 97
show 90
shower 10
shrimp 40
shrub 45
sick 91
side 79
sidewinder 27
sign 91
silk 91
silk kimono 91
silo 34
silverware 81
sing 91
sink 10, 52
six 64
sixty 64
size 68
size order 68
skate 47
skeleton 91
skin 8, 79, 89
skirt 22, 96
skull 91
sky 14, 92, 93, 104, 105
Sleeping Beauty 57
slide 27, 109
slow 92
small 67
smallest 68
smell 89
smock 18
snail 92
snake 7, 27, 79
snakes 7
sneaker 22, 28
sneakers 93
snowflakes 105
snowy 105
snowy day 105
soccer 92
soccer ball 9, 51
sock 22
socks 58
soft 66
solar panel 44
son 33
soup 41
South America 23, 39
South Carolina 100
South Dakota 100
space suit 8
spade foot toad 26
spend 92
spider 92
spine 91
sponge 21, 86
spoon 97
spoons 59
sports 92
spotted feathers 12
spring 88, 105
square 92
squash 40
squirrel 6, 27, 37
stamp 5
star 86, 93
stars 37, 93
state 17, 93
state capital 17, 93
state of California 93
states 100
station 62
steak 40
stem 8, 37, 75
stems 101
step stool 47
steps 44, 45
stethoscope 18

stick . . . 10
stool . . . 47
stop . . . 63
store . . . 35, 62, 63, 93
storm . . . 93
stormy . . . 105
stormy day . . . 105
story . . . 93
stove . . . 52, 65, 81
straight line . . . 55
strawberries . . . 40
strawberry . . . 35, 38
strawberry field . . . 35
street . . . 63
stretch . . . 93
string . . . 52
striped coat . . . 110, 111
stripes . . . 37, 74
strong . . . 94
student . . . 18, 54, 85
study . . . 94
suit . . . 8, 96
suitcase . . . 69
summer . . . 88, 105
sun . . . 25, 94
sun hat . . . 22
sunflower . . . 37, 88
sunflower seed . . . 88
sunglasses . . . 22
sunny . . . 104, 105
sunny day . . . 104
sunshine . . . 104
surprise . . . 94
surprised . . . 36
swallow . . . 12
sweater . . . 22
swim . . . 87, 94
swim fin . . . 87
swimsuit . . . 108
• **swing** . . . 94
swing set . . . 39
swinging . . . 71
syllable . . . 94

Tt

tadpoles . . . 20
tail . . . 12, 36, 53, 79, 110
take . . . 95
takes . . . 35
taking a walk . . . 71
talk . . . 95
tall . . . 95
Tallahassee . . . 17
tank . . . 87
tape measure . . . 59
tarantula . . . 27
taste . . . 89
teacher . . . 18, 54, 85, 94
team . . . 95
teddy bear . . . 46
teenager . . . 42
teeth . . . 33, 79, 109
telephone . . . 52
television . . . 55
ten . . . 60, 64
ten dollars . . . 60
Tennessee . . . 100
tennis shoes . . . 22
tent . . . 17
termite nest . . . 50
Texas . . . 100
thatched roof . . . 44
theater . . . 62, 63
thermometer . . . 91
things to do at the park . . . 71
think . . . 95
thirty . . . 64
thorax . . . 8
thousand . . . 64
thread . . . 89
three . . . 64
throw . . . 95
throwing a ball . . . 71
ticket . . . 33, 95
ticket booth . . . 33
tide pool . . . 88
• **tie** . . . 96
tiger . . . 57, 110
time . . . 96
tiny . . . 96
tire . . . 17, 96
title . . . 8, 14
toad . . . 26
today . . . 96, 105, 109
toddler . . . 42
toe . . . 13
toilet . . . 10
tomato . . . 52
tomatoes . . . 35
tomorrow . . . 96, 105
tonight . . . 96
tool . . . 97
tool belt . . . 18
toothbrush . . . 32
top . . . 14, 87, 98

tortillas 40
tortoise 27
touch 89
towel 10, 108
town 98
toy 24
toys 98
track 98
tracks 78
tractor 35
trade 98
traffic 21
train 78, 102
trash 71
trash can 71
tray 16, 80
tree 50, 75, 98, 111
trees 37, 60, 82
triangle 98
trombone 68
trowel 97
truck 19,35, 62, 102
trumpet 68
trunk 17, 75, 98, 110
tuba 68
tube 61, 87
tugboat 43, 102
tuna 41
tunnel 27, 98
turkey 34
turtle 7, 79
tusk 110
TV reporter 18
twenty 64
twig 48
two 64
type 98

Uu

umbrella 58, 78, 99
uncle 99
under 67
underground 99
underline 99
understand 99
understory 78
underwater 87
unhappy 99
United States 100
up 66
Utah 100

Vv

valentine 72, 101
valley 101
value 101
vase 101
vegetable 101
vegetables 35, 40
vehicle 102
veil 58
vendor 15
Vermont 100
vine 75
vines 50, 78
violin 68
Virginia 100
volume 59

Ww

waffles 41
wagon 20, 45
waiter 80
waitress 80
walk 71, 103
walrus 110
wand 57
want 103
warm 105
wash 103
washed 81
washing machine 56
Washington 100
waste 103
• **watch** 103
water 41, 61, 102, 103, 111
waterfall 103
watering can 61
watermelons 40
waves 93
weather 104, 105
web 92
webbed foot 12
week 16
weigh 106
weight 59
• **well** 106
went 81
West Virginia 100
wet 106
wheel 11, 73, 106
wheelchair 106

whipped cream 40
whisk 97
whisper 106
white fur 111
whole 72
wick 15
wide bill 12
wife 46
wild 106
windmill 31
window 45
windshield 17
windy 104
windy day 104
wing 12, 48
winner 106
winter 88, 105
Wisconsin 100
wise 107
wolf 57
woman 39, 72, 107
wood 15, 76
wood rat 26
wooden spoon 97
woodpecker 12
woods 7, 72
wool 108
word 64
words 75
worker 19
workers 19, 41, 35
world 107
worm 87
wren 26
wrench 19, 97
wrist 13, 76
wrist pad 76
wristband 103
write 107
Wyoming 100

Xx

x-ray 107
xylophone 107

Yy

yard 45, 108
yarn 108
yawn 108
year 108
yell 108
yellow 23
yellow lemon 23
yes 108
yesterday 109
yogurt 40
young woman 72
youngest 68
yucca 27

Zz

zebra 111
zero 109
zip 109
zipper 109
zoo 110

Acknowledgments

Every effort has been made to secure permission, but if any omissions have been made, please let us know.

Illustrations*

All illustrations by Roni Shepherd except for:
Ka Botzis, pp. 48 (4), 88 (1); **Ann Boyajian**, pp. 85 (3), 88 (3); **Drew-Brook-Cormack**, pp. 34 (1), 35 (5a–e); **Karen Dugan**, pp. 40 (2), 41 (1), 80 (2), 81 (5–8); **Theresa Flavin**, pp. 10 (1,5), 15 (1), 19 (5a–d), 45 (1,2), 52 (1), 55 (6), 57 (1a–d), 71 (2); **Loretta Krupinski**, pp. 6 (1), 7 (5a–e); **Fred Lynch**, pp. 62 (2), 63 (5), 102 (2); **Yoshi Miyake**, pp. 66 (1–8), 67 (1–8); **Carol Schwartz**, pp. 8 (1), 20 (6), 26 (2), 37 (7), 50 (2), 75 (1), 78 (7), 83 (1), 88 (7), 99 (5), 110 (2b), 111 (5); **Sandra T. Sevigny**, p. 91 (7); **Camille Venti**, pp. 14 (2), 16 (5b), 17 (7), 21 (5), 23 (1,3), 24 (4), 28 (1,2), 29 (3), 30 (7), 32 (3), 48 (1g;7), 53 (6), 54 (6), 55 (3), 64 (1,6), 70 (2,5), 72 (1,5,7), 74 (1c), 75 (5), 79 (2), 82 (4), 89 (5), 90 (1), 92 (8), 93 (7), 94 (8), 96 (3), 98 (1,6), 99 (6), 101 (2,3), 108 (6), 109 (1,6); **Elizabeth Wolf**, pp. 17 (4), 23 (6), 24 (1), 28 (7), 48 (8a), 58 (1), 61 (4), 93 (3), 100 (2,3), 104 (1), 105 (5–8).

Photography*

Animals, Animals: Ken Cole, p. 57 (5d); Harry Cutting, p. 6 (7); Richard Day, p. 7 (1); John Gerlach, pp. 12 (4), 25 (4); Joe McDonald, p. 12 (2a); Steven Miller, p. 12 (3); Fritz Prenzel, p. 6 (6); Leonard Lee Rue, p. 7 (3); Donald Specker, p. 98 (5); John Stevenson, p. 34 (7). **Artville:** pp. 8 (3a,c), 9 (3a,b;4b), 11 (7), 16 (4), 32 (2b), 60 (2a–c;3a–d), 90 (3), 97 (2). **Elinor Chamas:** p. 5 (6a–c). **Corbis-Bettmann:** UPI, p. 8 (7a). **Corel:** pp. 6 (3), 7 (2), 57 (5e), 87 (6,8). **Digital Stock:** pp. 9 (2,6), 14 (7), 16 (5a), 20 (1;2a), 36 (7), 37 (5a), 44 (5e), 51 (8), 53 (8), 60 (4), 62 (1), 64 (2), 70 (7a), 78 (6), 84 (8), 86 (1), 87 (5,7), 92 (4;5d), 93 (1), 94 (3,7), 95 (4,7), 96 (4,5), 99 (3), 101 (5), 104 (3), 106 (7), 107 (3). **Bill Eichner:** p. 107 (1). **Envision:** Steven Needham, p. 31 (1). **Image Club:** pp. 8 (3b), 31 (6), 32 (2a), 51 (3a,b), 56 (4a,b), 59 (3), 75 (6a,b), 83 (6), 84 (6a), 97 (3), 103 (6). **The Image Works:** p. 9 (8), Esbin/Anderson, pp. 59 (4), 101 (3); M. Antman, p. 15 (5); Stuart Cohen, p. 89 (2e); J. Crawford, p. 64 (5); Bob Daemmrich, pp. 16 (3), 18 (9), 28 (4), 29 (1), 32 (5), 42 (5), 44 (3), 51 (5), 88 (6), 91 (6), 104 (1); Sonda Dawes, p. 28 (3); Edrington, p. 38 (2); Fujifotos, p. 41 (7); Jeff Greenberg, pp. 88 (5), 34 (3); David Hall, p. 86 (10); J. Marshall, p. 37 (6); Okoniewski, p. 92 (1); K. Preuss, p. 103 (7); N. Richmond, pp. 99 (8), 106 (2); M Siluk, p. 85 (5a); Skjold, p. 59 (2); Joe Sohm, pp. 44 (5f), 90 (4), 92 (5b); Spratt, p. 89 (2d). **International Stock:** Robert Arakaki: p. 41 (5), Laurie Bayer, p. 61 (7); Bob Jacobson, p. 57 (8); Earl Kogler, p. 52 (8); S. Meyers, p. 52 (4); John Michael, p. 58 (7); John V Neal, p. 53 (3a); KH Photo, p. 44 (5a); Michael Paras, p. 54 (5); Rae Russel, p. 51 (6b); Elliott Smith, p. 53 (5); Bill Stanton, p. 33 (7). **Bonnie Kamin:** pxp. 5 (2), 10 (7), 14 (3), 30 (5), 54 (3), 56 (3), 59 (1), 60 (1), 69 (4), 82 (7), 97 (5), 107 (8). **Metaphoto:** pp. 37 (1), 59 (5), 100 (1). **Lawrence Migdale:** pp. 25 (7), 36 (6), 54 (8), 58 (6). **Monkmeyer:** p. 86 (2), Dollarhide, pp. 90 (7), 110 (1); Forbert, p. 43 (3); Forsyth, p. 84 (4); Gish, p. 83 (2); Goodwin, pp. 24 (2), 71 (1); Gottlieb, p. 74 (5); Grantpix, p. 14 (5); Debra P. Hershkowitz, p. 48 (6); LeDuc, p. 18 (5); Merrim, p. 74 (1b); Murray, p. 77 (7); Shackman, p. 76 (8); Sidney, p. 84 (5); Yin, pp. 86 (2,); Zimbel, p. 73 (1). **Peter Arnold, Inc:** Fritz Polking, p. 11 (5). **Photo Edit:** Bill Aron, pp. 41 (6), 92 (2), 97 (1); Billy E. Barnes, p. 106 (8); Robert Brenner, pp. 21 (3), 83 (4); Paul Conklin, pp. 42 (7), 72 (8), 108 (3); Deborah Davis, p. 25 (2); Amy C. Etra, p. 106 (3); Myrleen Ferguson, pp. 17 (2), 20 (7), 22 (4), 73 (8), 76 (3), 82 (2), 84 (3), 85 (5c), 91 (1), 95 (5); Tony Freeman, pp. 10 (3), 17 (5), 32 (4), 49 (5), 74 (1a), 76 (1,7), 79 (3), 89 (2b), 90 (2), 94 (2); Spencer Grant, p. 41 (8a); Jeff Greenberg, pp. 70 (7c), 74 (3), 78 (4); Richard Hutchings, p. 18 (2); Felicia Martinez, p. 108 (2); Phil McCarten, p. 53 (3b); Tom McCarthy, pp. 44 (4), 11 (8); John Neubauer, p. 49 (6); Michael Newman, pp. 30 (6), 47 (4), 56 (2), 82 (8), 88 (8), 89 (2a), 102 (1); J. Nourok, p. 72 (4); Alan Oddie, p. 21 (6); A. Ramey, p. 93 (6); Elena Rooraid, p. 70 (3a); Robin L. Sachs, p. 22 (7); Nancy Sheehan, pp. 17 (1), 22 (5), 77 (8), 106 (4); W.B. Spunbarg, p. 17 (8); Barbara Stitzer, p. 47 (2); Rudi Von Briel, p. 98 (2); Dana White, p. 39 (2); David Young-Wolff, pp. 18 (11), 23 (7), 29 (5), 36 (4), 42 (1,8), 49 (7), 55 (4), 72 (6), 73 (4b), 76 (5), 78 (2), 83 (7), 85 (2), 89 (2c;8), 92 (5a;5c), 98 (3), 101 (6g); Elizabeth Zuckerman, p. 109 (7). **Photo Researchers:** Mark Boulton, p. 79 (6d); A. Carrara, p. 48 (1c); Ken Cavanagh, p. 43 (7); Tim Davis, p. 28 (8); Alan Evrard, p. 70 (3b); A.u.H-F Michler/ OKAPIA, p. 82 (6); Jerry L. Ferrara, p. 27 (2); Tony Franceschi, p. 65 (3); Adam Jones, p. 108 (4); Craig K. Lorenz, p. 27 (4); Tom McHugh, p. 27 (1,3); Lawrence Migdale, p. 75 (6c); Margaret Miller, p. 69 (5); Rod Planck, p. 48 (1e); Carl Purcell, p. 104 (2); Leonard Lee Rue, p. 50 (1); Blair Seitz, pp. 21 (7), 106 (1); Lee F. Snyder, p. 18 (12); Joe Sohm, p. 29 (2); Camille Tokerud, p. 46 (2); Stan Wayman, p. 44 (1); David Weintraub, p. 53 (2); Jim Zipp, p. 103 (8). **PhotoDisc:** pp. 5 (7), 6 (4a,b), 6 (5a,b), 10 (4), 12 (2b), 13 (1,2), 20 (2b), 21 (8), 22 (1,4), 23 (4a,b;5), 24 (5), 26 (1), 29 (6), 31 (1b), 34 (2,4,6,8), 35 (1–9), 36 (1a–e), 37 (5b), 38 (5;6a,b), 39 (5,7), 43 (5), 44 (2), 46 (8), 47 (6;7a,b), 48 (5), 49 (2,4,8), 51 (4), 55 (8), 56 (8), 57 (5a,b), 59 (7), 60 (7), 65 (2), 68 (3a–d), 70 (7b), 73 (3;4a;6), 74 (2,4), 75 (8), 79 (1;6a–c), 83 (3), 84 (6b), 85 (5b), 89 (6), 91 (2a–c), 93 (8), 101 (6c–f), 106 (5), 107 (4). **Picture Perfect:** pp. 15 (4,7). **Stockbyte:** pp. 8 (5), 31 (8), 37 (2;3a–d,f), 44 (5b), 64 (4), 70 (1), 97 (4), 101 (6a,b). **The Stock Market:** George W. Disario, p. 107 (2); Ronnie Kaufman, p. 8 (4). **SuperStock:** pp. 6 (8), 7 (4), 8 (8), 9 (4a;5), 12 (7,8), 15 (6), 18 (1,4), 20 (4), 29 (4), 39 (3), 40 (1), 44 (5d), 46 (1,3,5), 74 (7), 82 (5), 85 (4), 86 (4,7,10), 91 (5), 98 (7), 103 (2). **Tony Stone Images:** Gregg Adams, p. 104 (5); Kim Blaxland, p. 104 (4); Peter Cade, p. 52 (3); Myrleen Cate, p. 60 (8); Chris Cheadle, p. 91 (2e); Ed Collacott, p. 104 (6); Daniel Cox, p. 12 (1); Paul Harris, p. 51 (6a); Derke O'Hare, p. 61 (5); David Oliver, p. 108 (7); Rick Rushing, p. 80 (1); Frank Siteman, p. 76 (4); Kalunzy Thatch, p. 58 (5); David Young-Wolff, pp. 73 (5), 78 (3). **Uniphoto:** pp. 5 (4), 69 (2), 107 (7); Rhonda Bishop, p. 57 (5c); Rick Brady, p. 21 (2); Matt Brown, p. 18 (6); Paul Conklin, p. 32 (1); Bob Daemmrich, pp. 17 (3), 58 (3), 78 (5), 94 (1,5); Ben Garacci, p. 109 (8); Charles Gupton, p. 28 (5); Bob Llewellyn, pp. 68 (1), 18 (3), 54 (1); Jeffry W Myers, p. 85 (5d); Shaun van Steyn, p. 20 (3). **Tracy Wheeler:** pp. 59 (6), 96 (1). **Beth Whitney:** pp. 18 (10), 24 (8), 41 (8b), 44 (5c), 58 (4). **Liz Garza Williams:** p. 33 (2).

***Credits:** Illustrations and photo credits are identified by cell number (1-8) and positioned within the cell (a-z), in top to bottom order.

1	5
2	6
3	7
4	8